The Power of
Ethical Persuasion

The Power of Ethical Persuasion

of Ethical Persuasion

From Conflict to Partnership at Work and in Private Life

Tom Rusk, M.D.

with D. Patrick Miller

VIKING

VIKING
Published by the Penguin Group
Penguin Books USA Inc., 375 Hudson Street,
New York, New York 10014, U.S.A.
Penguin Books Ltd, 27 Wrights Lane,
London W8 5TZ, England
Penguin Books Australia Ltd, Ringwood,
Victoria, Australia
Penguin Books Canada Ltd, 10 Alcorn Avenue,
Toronto, Ontario, Canada M4V 3B2
Penguin Books (N.Z.) Ltd, 182–190 Wairau Road,
Auckland 10, New Zealand

Penguin Books Ltd, Registered Offices:
Harmondsworth, Middlesex, England

First published in 1993 by Viking Penguin,
a division of Penguin Books USA Inc.

1 2 3 4 5 6 7 8 9 10

Grateful acknowledgment is made for permission to reprint
excerpts from the following copyrighted works:
"Emotional Impact," by Margie Patlak, *Los Angeles Times,*
June 24, 1991. By permission of the author.
"Out of Africa and into the Wilds of America's Corporate
Jungles," by Tony Perry, *Los Angeles Times,* May 3, 1992. Copyright, 1992,
Los Angeles Times. Reprinted by permission.

LIBRARY OF CONGRESS CATALOGING IN PUBLICATION DATA
Rusk, Tom.
The power of ethical persuasion: winning through understanding in
difficult communications/Tom Rusk with D. Patrick Miller.
p.   cm.
Includes index.
ISBN 0-670-84617-1
1. Negotiation.   2. Persuasion (Psychology)   3. Interpersonal
conflict.   I. Miller, D. Patrick, 1953–   .   II. Title.
BF637.N4R87   1993
158'.5—dc20   92-50385

Printed in the United States of America
Set in Bembo
Designed by Ann Gold

To Judy, for everything,
but especially for her faith in me

Acknowledgments

I must begin by explaining how Patrick Miller, my co-author, and I worked together to create this book. Patrick's writing seems as connected to my mind as my own speech. He describes and explains my experiences, ideas, and feelings in writing better than I have ever heard them from my own lips. During the writing of this and our previous book, we talked (mostly by telephone) for hours on end, at least three for every chapter, not including our conversational excursions into mutually diverting side trips. All these conversations he recorded and transcribed. In addition I would send him my notes, handouts, and copies of transparencies from workshops, along with some underlined and annotated books and articles of other authors that have been seminal for me.

Somehow he brought all the material together and conveyed my ideas with more clarity and coherence than I dreamed possible. I would impatiently await each draft of a chapter to see what new magic he had performed. The most interesting parts of the entire process were occasions when we would practice Ethical Persuasion ourselves in order to negotiate our rare differences in perspective, strategy, or tactics. I realize Patrick is a gift from God to me, and I could have used some of his art to adequately convey in writing my gratitude.

Both Patrick and I want to express our appreciation and indebtedness to those who generously donated their time and energy to the task of critically reading the chapter drafts as they were generated: Ann Lyon-Boutelle, John S. and Robin M. Davis, Laurie Fox, Leonard Goodstein, Suzanne Hess, Marguerite Jackson, Natalie Rusk, and Richard Salter. Their perspectives were extremely helpful in forging the final manuscript. Most tried out the Ethical Persuasion process in their day-to-day lives, and their comments about these experiences were especially useful.

Although acknowledgments are written before much of the editor's work is done, I want to express now my heartfelt appreciation for Caroline White's early and unflagging support of this project. She and her colleagues at Viking have been so gracious and enthusiastic about this book's message and Patrick's writing that I have begun to risk believing wholeheartedly in it myself.

It requires a flexible and sophisticated agent to sell a book to a major publisher. Fortunately we have that in the Linda Chester Literary Agency. Linda Chester and Laurie Fox made certain our proposal received the fullest consideration and ultimately a wonderful home.

Finally, I again wish to let Jan Falldorf, my secretary for almost twenty years, know how much her help and calm presence have meant to me.

Alpine, California

Contents

Preface

This book teaches a practical method for increasing one's influence in difficult, emotionally charged communications by leading the way toward greater mutual understanding. Ethical Persuasion (EP) will help you settle arguments, solve problems, and ease negotiations in the short term, but it will also help you deepen any kind of relationship over the long term.

The "persuasion" of this method is not the usual sort, in which one person convinces another of the rightness of his viewpoint or the worth of the goods he's selling. EP is an approach that persuades people to treat each other with greater respect, understanding, caring, and fairness. This method is equally applicable to intimate relationships, friendships, families, and professional environments.

Ethical Persuasion surpasses other problem-solving and negotiation strategies by helping people communicate to each other what it *feels* like to live in their separate, private worlds of experience. Whenever people can make that kind of connection, resolving their differences and reaching creative, practical agreements becomes much easier. But the long-term benefits of deeper intimacy, insight, and compassion are even more significant.

The inspiration for developing Ethical Persuasion arose mainly from my own need to communicate better with my family, friends, and clients, and to undo my particular habits of isolation, aggression, and self-denial. Thus, all the people who have tried to understand me, help me accept myself, and help me understand and accept them have had a hand in the design of this method.

Phase 1 of EP, "Exploring the Other Person's Viewpoint," is strongly influenced by the thinking and personal example of the late great psychologist Carl Rogers. Phase 2, "Explaining Your Viewpoint," is more subtly influenced by the legacy of business-management guru Peter Drucker. The third and final EP phase, "Creating Resolutions," is a collection of tried-and-true problem-solving strategies in a new synthesis.

Many contemporary approaches to negotiation and communication use one or more steps of the Ethical Persuasion methodology; I didn't invent the ideas of careful listening, restating others' viewpoints, or confirming mutual understanding. What I hope I have achieved in this book is a simple yet powerful combination of these techniques, founded on a deeper understanding than has been previously described of the role of feelings in difficult communications. Strong feelings (and their passionate expression) often prevent us from achieving mutual understanding. Yet when usefully interpreted and managed, feelings can vastly accelerate and deepen our connections to each other, for they arise from the inner world of our shared human spirit.

Lastly, I have tried to describe how the values of *respect, understanding, caring,* and *fairness* can reconnect and anchor our feelings to our inner spirit and ethically guide the conduct of sensitive communications. You don't have to understand fully the interplay of values and feelings *before* you can try Ethical Persuasion. But to follow the steps of EP without sincerely pursuing the healthy integration of values and feelings within yourself would be to execute an empty, meaningless technique. You might as well keep on arguing.

Ethical Persuasion is an outgrowth of the psychological counseling mode I call "guided self-change," described at length in my most recent previous book, *Instead of Therapy: Help Yourself Change and Change the Help You're Getting.* Although I am a board-certified psychiatrist, I have not practiced conventional psychotherapy for some years now, preferring to coach my counseling clients on the most rapid routes toward constructive personal change that they can devise for themselves. I introduce them to EP by modeling it in my guided self-change counseling, and I also teach EP to executives, managers, and employees of businesses, public service concerns, and government institutions.

Like some recent critics of conventional therapy, I believe that it can encourage people to become too wrapped up in their past and their private problems, at the serious cost of obstructing their capacity to change their lives for the better in the here and now. By contrast, guided self-change encourages people to experiment with new, *value-driven* beliefs and behaviors at every opportunity. Learning

Ethical Persuasion helps clients express and explore their commitment to personal change in their everyday relationships with friends, intimates, family, and co-workers. Thus EP can provide a vital interface for personal, social, and political change. EP is not just another way of talking *about* change; it's a way to change yourself and ethically influence others while you're talking.

As the author of this book, I am responsible for its contents. However, I owe its style and much of its organization to my collaborator and wordsmith, D. Patrick Miller. As an independent writer in the "journalism of consciousness" who contributes to a wide variety of periodicals, Patrick specializes in the investigation of psychological and spiritual subject matter that is often ignored or misinterpreted by the mainstream press. His interests and experience have dovetailed miraculously with my own in the creation of this and my previous book. Even before he had heard of Ethical Persuasion, Patrick was applying a similar philosophy to his own reporting—for instance, allowing his interview subjects to read and comment on the articles quoting them before publication. (This is the opposite of standard journalistic practice, in which interview subjects cannot see how their quotes and ideas are used in an article until after it is in print, often leaving them feeling they have been misunderstood or unfairly treated.) My collaboration with Patrick has been a fruitful experiment in mutual learning, blessed with a remarkable lack of stress or conflict.

We have one joint apology to make to readers. At certain times (especially in the book's midsection) it was frequently necessary to follow singular antecedents such as "a person" or "someone" with plural references like "they," "their," "them," and so on. This was done to avoid littering the manuscript with the phrases "him or her" and "his or hers," and we hope it's not too offensive to those who are sticklers for grammatical propriety. Elsewhere, we have alternated gender references (he, she, her, his) in a way that seemed natural to us.

Perhaps you have picked up this book because you share some of my fervent hope and belief that people are capable of making a quantum leap in learning to understand each other and themselves—and thence to solving our many daunting problems with greater speed and efficiency. If Ethical Persuasion helps you to take a single step toward that leap, then all the study, preparation, and struggle to craft this method and this book have been worthwhile.

Tom Rusk, M.D.
Alpine, California
September 1992

The Three Phases of Ethical Persuasion

PHASE 1: EXPLORING THE OTHER PERSON'S VIEWPOINT

The Seven Steps of Exploring the Other Person's Viewpoint

1. Establish that your immediate goal is mutual understanding, not problem solving.
2. Elicit the other person's thoughts, feelings, and desires about the subject at hand.
3. Ask for the other person's help in understanding him or her. Try not to defend or disagree.
4. Repeat the other person's position in your own words to show you understand.
5. Ask the other person to correct your understanding and keep restating his or her position.
6. Refer back to your position only to keep things going.
7. Repeat steps 1 through 6 until the other person unreservedly agrees that you understand his or her position.

PHASE 2: EXPLAINING YOUR VIEWPOINT

The Five Steps of Explaining Your Viewpoint

1. Ask for a fair hearing in return.
2. Begin with an explanation of how the other person's thoughts and feelings affect you. Avoid blaming and self-defense as much as possible.

3. Carefully explain your thoughts, desires, and feelings as *your* truth, not *the* truth.
4. Ask for restatements of your position—and corrections of any factual inaccuracies—as necessary.
5. Review your respective positions.

PHASE 3: CREATING RESOLUTIONS

The Three Steps (Plus Options) *of Creating Resolutions*

1. Affirm your mutual understanding and confirm that you are both ready to consider options for resolution.
2. Brainstorm multiple options.
3. If a mutually agreeable solution is not yet obvious, try one or more of the following options:
   - Take time out to reconsider, consult, exchange proposals, and reconvene.
   - Agree to neutral arbitration, mediation, or counseling.
   - Compromise between alternate solutions.
   - "Take turns" between alternate solutions.
   - Yield (for now) once your position is thoroughly and respectfully considered.
   - Assert your positional power after thoroughly and respectfully considering their position.
   - Agree to disagree and still respect each other; then, if you can, go your separate ways on the particular issue.

Part I

The Roots of Ethical Persuasion

This book teaches a new way of handling difficult communications. It's not a grab bag of special tricks or manipulative techniques that will get you what you want without any compromise or extra effort. Instead, this book proposes that changing your communications for the better requires changing yourself for the better. Ethical Persuasion helps you achieve both kinds of change simultaneously, but it requires courage, patience, and lots of practice. If you want to get the greatest value possible from this book, then get ready to go to work on the very next page.

Even though Part I is not the "how-to" section of the book, it presents a number of mental exercises and provocative ideas that require your serious involvement. Chapter 1 examines five common barriers to human understanding and presents three scripted dialogues that end in conflict and separation. (In Part III, you'll see how each of these arguments could be constructively "rerouted" or resumed with the use of EP.) Chapters 2 and 3 present valuable information on feelings and values, providing an essential foundation for learning the technique of EP, which is presented in Part II.

1

Why Does Communication Break Down?

Can you remember the last time you had an important conversation that broke down into an unproductive, painful argument? Or one that ended with someone's retreat into a bitter silence? Was it at work with your boss, a colleague, or a subordinate? Perhaps it was a quarrel with one of your children, or a parent, spouse, lover, or friend. Please take a moment to recall a recent, specific situation.

Do you recall the moment in your chosen conversation when things first seemed to go wrong—and when it became obvious that a mutual understanding would not be reached?

Try to bring back the feelings you experienced during this crucial moment. Did you begin to feel resentful or righteous, abandoned or abused, vicious or victimized? As the situation intensified, did you feel totally in the right, and determined to win the argument no matter what? Or did you feel on the defensive—hurt and hopelessly confused, fed up and furious? Perhaps you were surprised and irritated at how upset the other person became over something that seemed so minor. Or were you distressed by how callous he or she could be about something that felt very important to you?

When you have recaptured some of the emotions from that last conflict, hold on to them for a moment. Then, however uncomfortable these feelings may be, try to stand back and make use of the unique human capacity to observe yourself. Carefully reviewing the feelings stirred up inside yourself by that difficult situation, try to appreciate the sheer energy your feelings carried (apart from whether they seemed "good" or "bad," justified or inappropriate). See whether you can feel any acceptance of your feelings from this objective but compassionate viewpoint—as if you were observing some other upset person who is very close to you.

Now take a moment to consider the actual person with whom you were arguing. Keeping your own strong feelings in mind, imagine that he or she may have been experiencing equally strong feelings, whether or not they were obvious on the surface. Try to recognize and appreciate the power of the other person's feelings. Leave "right" or "wrong" out of the picture for the moment. Simply try to sense the flow of authentic, intense, and perhaps out-of-control feelings going on within and between two human beings. See if you can appreciate both the discomfort and the vitality of the entire situation.

If your idea about what was happening in your last

argument is changing, then you've begun to grasp a fundamental principle of the communication technique I call Ethical Persuasion (EP). This book will teach you how to apply the three phases of EP to all kinds of crucial communications, helping you learn to prevent arguments, restore respectful communication after unavoidable conflicts, solve problems, and achieve a greater understanding of human beings than you may now think possible.

A Strategic Application of the Golden Rule

It's mysterious and ironic that after millions of years of evolution—and a hundred or so of modern psychological theorizing and research—we human beings have not advanced very far in person-to-person communications. We can generally exchange thoughts and ideas pretty well, but nonetheless we often fail to *understand* each other. For the most part, what we fail to communicate clearly is our feelings, those nonverbal, deeply rooted energies that can lead us to act in contradiction to our will and our rational decisions. Between people, strong feelings can easily escalate a simple misunderstanding into a senseless battle of wills. Even wars between nations have begun that way.

Modern psychology has done relatively little to help us comprehend our feelings, or learn to manage them in accordance with the fundamental values of *respect, understanding, caring,* and *fairness* in order to create happier, more fulfilling lives.* Many successful books on communication

* A full analysis of the shortcomings of conventional psychology and psychotherapy can be found in my book *Instead of Therapy: Help Yourself Change and Change the Help You're Getting* (Hay House, 1991).

strategies have sought to teach people how to expedite problem solving or gain the upper hand in all kinds of negotiations. But these strategies almost always ignore the power of feelings in all kinds of relationships, and the need to uphold explicit social values in the conduct of human communication.

As far as I'm concerned, there never was or will be a better basic communication strategy than the Golden Rule: *Do unto others as you would have them do unto you.* Ethical Persuasion is a practical, strategic method of applying the Golden Rule to every kind of important communication —not as a means of merely doing a "good deed," but as a means of giving everyone a fair hearing, creating the optimal solutions for thorny problems, and fostering long-term, trusting relationships. You might say that EP is a technique for learning to "respect others' feelings as you would have them respect your own." That's not all it does—but it's a good introduction.

I must admit that Ethical Persuasion is not an easy or instinctive thing to do. Neither is the Golden Rule, when actually applied rather than merely stitched in needlepoint. Both of these strategies are doable, however—and they both offer enormous payoffs in understanding, cooperation, creativity, and inner and outer peace.

Five Kinds of Difficulty

What usually goes wrong in human communications is nobody's fault and everybody's problem. At its root, the problem is the ever-present paradox of the human condition: *our survival and security seem to depend on self-defense, but understanding, cooperation, and closeness require that we risk vulnerability*. All human communication—whether between children at play or diplomats trying to avert war—reflects this push-and-pull tension between self-protection and openness. As husbands and wives, parents and children, bosses, subordinates, and partners, we often avoid saying what we really think and feel for fear of provoking each other. We defend this habit by saying that we don't want to damage our relationships. Yet it's exactly this withholding that interferes with the openness necessary to create closeness.

The struggle between self-defense and vulnerability can be viewed in terms of five interrelated factors.

Five Barriers to Human Communication

1. We all live in *unique and private worlds* of personal experience.
2. Nearly everyone is insecure to some extent. Thus, when we feel threatened, hurt, or angry, we tend to react with *blame and self-defense* rather than attempts to improve communication.
3. Everyone has *difficulty handling strong feelings* and maintaining a dynamic balance between mind and heart.
4. *Feelings are facts* to the person experiencing them. Rejecting a person's feelings makes the person feel rejected as a whole.
5. We almost always perceive some kind of power imbalance in difficult communications, but *we rarely discuss issues of power openly.*

As you read the three dialogues that follow, it will be helpful to keep these five barriers in mind. As you read and review each dialogue, ask yourself:

1. To what extent do the participants acknowledge and respect each other's unique point of view? Are they always willing to learn something new about each other's worlds of personal experience?
2. Is anyone willing to admit fear or insecurity as a means of improving understanding? When do they resort to blaming others or defending themselves instead?
3. When do strong feelings seem to interfere with the participants' ability to be reasonable and considerate?
4. Are the participants more engaged in determining "right" and "wrong" than in respecting each other's feelings and viewpoints?
5. Do the participants respectfully discuss any real or perceived imbalances of power in their relationship?

Three Conflicts

The first of the following conversations occurs within an intimate relationship, the second in a business environment, and the third in a family context. When each of these conversations is rerouted in Part III (the first in Chapter 7, the second in Chapter 8, and the third in Chapter 9) the application of EP to each of these arenas of human communication will be discussed in full. As you read each of the following dialogues, keep an eye out for what goes wrong in each one. Try not to take sides, however. (And take note of how difficult such objectivity is!) Instead, imagine that every person in these conversations is a close friend, someone you really care about.

(NOTE: If you're curious, feel free to skip ahead and read the second versions of these dialogues right after the first versions. This will give you a feel for EP even before you've studied its philosophy and method in detail. Reading the second versions again later will yield deeper insights into the process of improving human communication.)

1. Control vs. Commitment

A frank, independent woman in her midthirties, Gail makes her living as a self-employed physical fitness consultant for corporations. She's been a registered nurse for over ten years, but she hasn't worked in a hospital since her divorce from an older doctor seven years ago, at his instigation. Since then, going it alone in her emotional life and business has suited Gail just fine. She's wary of personal or professional involvements that might threaten her independence or cause her pain. She doesn't like the idea of letting anyone else have too much control of her life.

Nine months ago, Gail began dating Perry, a quiet, self-effacing man she's been seeing a few times a month ever since. Perry is also divorced, but he coparents two preteen children. He gets along reasonably well with his ex-wife, Sharon, but Gail thinks he gives in to Sharon too much. Though Perry and Gail seem to be getting closer, they haven't talked seriously about any plans for the future. She likes his kids, but she wouldn't want to be a parent to them. She'd rather start a family of her own, if she's going to have one.

All the uncertainties of their relationship have been swirling around in Gail's head for the last few weeks, so she's looking forward to a long weekend with Perry to talk things over. A three-day trip for just the two of them is a rarity, given their different work schedules and Perry's time commitment to his children. On a Wednesday evening, Gail is in a buoyant mood as she looks through her closet and begins to make decisions about what clothes to take for the trip on Friday morning. When the phone rings, she figures that it's probably Perry calling to ask what *he* should wear. . . .

PERRY: Hi, honey. You certainly sound like you're in a good mood.

GAIL: [*Chuckling*] Well, I was just going through my clothes for our trip when you called, and when the phone rang I just knew it was you. Do you want me to go through your closet, too?

PERRY: [*Laughing uneasily*] Well, I guess you know me pretty well by now: wardrobe is not my strong point. If I had five copies of my gray suit for the office, I'd be set for life. . . . But I *am* calling about the trip, honey. A little problem has come up.

GAIL: What kind of problem?

PERRY: Well, you remember that I had this weekend open because the kids were supposed to go see their cousins?

GAIL: They were going to stay with your sister Charlotte.

PERRY: Right. Well, her kids are both coming down with the flu or something. Anyway, nobody's having any fun over there, so the big reunion of the cousins is off. . . . So, uh, it's still my turn with the kids.

GAIL: What do you mean, Perry?

PERRY: I mean they have to be with me for the long weekend. It would have been my turn anyway except that they—

GAIL: But Perry, we've had this planned for weeks! Can't Sharon take care of them?

PERRY: Well, honey, you know Sharon and I have this visitation agreement, and she made plans, too. I hate to ask her to change her plans around when it's not her turn.

GAIL: But did you?

PERRY: Did I what?

GAIL: Did you ask Sharon if she could change her plans?

PERRY: No, not exactly. I told her you and I were really looking forward to this trip, but you know . . . it's just not her concern. I mean, I have to be fair.

GAIL: How about being fair to me? Don't I get some consideration? I'm getting a little tired of the feeling that you just squeeze me in when it's no trouble for Sharon or the kids.

PERRY: Honey, you know it's not like that. Listen, we can still take the trip. You know it's okay with Sharon if we take the kids with us. . . .

GAIL: To a *bed-and-breakfast,* Perry? I don't think so.

PERRY: Well, I know it can't be exactly the same trip, Gail. We can all go to—

GAIL: No, we will not *all* go anywhere, Perry. You know I like your kids, and I respect that they're a big part of your life. But we made plans for a long weekend *alone,* Perry, and I really wanted that to happen.

PERRY: Well, there will be lots of weekends we can be together. Look, this is just a little glitch that has to be ironed out. Please be reasonable! Let's try to think of a place the four of us can go, maybe where the kids will keep themselves busy, and you and I can—

GAIL: [*Beginning to cry*] No, Perry—no! This is *not* just a little glitch to me! It's the same old thing—Sharon and the kids always come first! You don't even have the guts to *ask* Sharon if she'll do you a favor for a change—I guess you don't want to give her the idea I might be really important to you.

PERRY: Hey, now, you know that isn't true—

GAIL: Do I, Perry? Do I? Maybe we don't need to talk about us after all. Maybe everything is perfectly clear already. Just go take care of your kids, okay? But leave me *alone!* [*Slams down the phone*]

Conflicts in intimate adult relationships can be exceptionally bitter and disheartening because we expect so much of our love partnerships. The early romantic phase of seemingly perfect harmony inevitably passes, and soon we must negotiate divergent goals, differences between the male and female ways of self-expression and relating, and power issues that everyone finds it very difficult to bring out into the open. In Chapter 7 you'll see how this conversation between Gail and Perry could go better if Perry makes use of Ethical Persuasion in place of his habit of passive manipulation.

2. When Politics Get Personal

At fifty-nine, Martin is a secure and confident personnel manager for a business computer firm. He's spent ten years overseeing the staffing of a network of retail outlets, and he's proud that not one of them has closed despite the overcompetitive computer marketplace and the recent economic downturn. It's widely acknowledged in the firm that his selection of bright, dependable store managers has made a tremendous difference, and his authority is now virtually unchallenged. In fact, he won an important award at the firm's last annual dinner, and the CEO publicly complimented him on having a "magic touch" with hiring, firing, and promotions.

That doesn't mean his job is easy. It takes a lot of footwork, networking, head-hunting, and hand holding. And occasionally he has to make tough decisions. Last week at one of the company's most profitable financial district stores, two assistant managers with very different qualifications came up for promotion to the manager's slot. One is Doug, a thirty-six-year-old white man with only a high-school diploma but ten solid years in the company; the other is Lenora, a very sharp twenty-seven-year-old African-American woman with university honors in her résumé but only a couple of years with the company, all in one store.

Lenora is a hard worker and would have looked very good for the firm in terms of affirmative action, but Martin feels she has a lot of negatives. Young and comparatively inexperienced, she seems to Martin to be carrying a sizable chip on her shoulder. As part of an all-white upper management team, Martin favors greater minority representation in the firm but has to admit to himself that he is a little uneasy about a black woman running the whole show in a financial district store. He just can't be sure if the predominantly white male clientele would be ready for it. Sales could slide.

So, with considerable hesitation, Martin has selected Doug, a company veteran of long personal acquaintance. Doug isn't what Martin would call brilliant, but he can do the job. He is always very responsive to corporate direction and doesn't have any strong negatives.

It is Martin's policy to call each of the people in competition for a position into his office—the loser first—to explain his decision before an announcement is made. But when Doug called about an unrelated matter yesterday, Martin let the news slip—a regrettable mistake. No doubt that's why Lenora is on his appointment list this morning. She has reason to be unhappy, and Martin promises himself to make it up to her—he just doesn't know how. When his secretary announces that Lenora is in the outer office, Martin knows that his peacemaking skills will be stretched to the limit. . . .

MARTIN: [*To his secretary*] Tell Lenora to come on in.

LENORA: [*Entering, speaking brusquely*] Good morning, Mr. Swanson.

MARTIN: Have a seat, Lenora. Since when did you start calling me Mr. Swanson?

LENORA: [*Remains standing*] Since you decided you could treat me like a nobody, Mr. Swanson. I learned about Doug's promotion from a *floor clerk* yesterday afternoon, and I—

MARTIN: [*Flustered*] Now, Lenora, I admit that I owe you an apology. You deserved a private meeting over this decision—it was a very tough one, you should know that—and, well, I just slipped up. I've known Doug a long time, and when he happened to call yesterday . . . What can I say? I've never been great at keeping secrets.

LENORA: Yes, that's easy to believe. I feel like a fool! I should have realized that I was never *really* in the running for this promotion. You were just putting on a show, pretending you might make a black woman manager. But when the show's over, you say, "Just kidding, folks!" and give your old pal Doug the nudge. Like he didn't already know. . . .

MARTIN: Lenora, that is completely unfair and you know it. I had a lot of factors to consider in this decision, and

I'll be happy to lay them all out for you if you want to know how I made my choice. You might not agree with my reasoning, but I can assure you that this promotion was not a foregone conclusion. You certainly have a lot going for you, Lenora, and your time will come, I assure you. Look, I owe you one for handling this badly. Why don't you sit down so we can discuss this calmly.

LENORA: I didn't come here to discuss things calmly, Mr. Swanson. I came here to let you know I *won't* sit down for this. I want you to know that I'm prepared to call my lawyer and file a discrimination complaint. But, unlike you, I'm not going behind your back. You're finding out from *me*, not your secretary.

MARTIN: [*Obviously shocked*] Now, wait a minute, young lady. You may be upset, but you can't just come in here and threaten me. You call a lawyer and you'll be out of this company before he can say good morning and charge you five hundred dollars for it!

LENORA: That's just fine, Mr. Swanson. I'll pay my money and take my chances, because I don't want to stay where I'm treated like this. But you should know I can raise an awful lot of hell on my way out the door, Mr. *Award Winner*. [*Turns toward the door*]

MARTIN: [*Angrily*] You go right ahead and do that, Miss Diamond. Be my guest! But don't expect *me* to show you out!

[*Lenora leaves, and Martin raises his hands toward the ceiling in frustration.*]

When individuals find themselves in conflicts with broad social and political overtones, their personal exchange can be overwhelmed rapidly by issues that are too big for them to negotiate in the moment. In Chapter 8 you'll see how Lenora "rehabilitates" the situation with her supervisor by writing him a letter that reopens their dialogue. Then Ethical Persuasion will help her maximize her personal power not only to repair her relationship with Martin, but to take it to a much higher and more productive level.

3. A Declaration of Independence

Lisa is a good-natured and sociable suburban fifteen-year-old. She gets along pretty well with her parents, Gene and Peg, and shakes her head in disbelief at some of the terrible stories her friends tell about their parents, who are either too strict, or not getting along with each other, or just completely out of touch with their kids. She's very glad that her folks aren't heavy drinkers or working all the time, and that they let her hang out with her girlfriends without prying or making a lot of rules. In fact, Lisa's friends like to spend time at her house because her parents are so laid back. She adores her older brother, Greg, who just started college, and he's always confirmed that their parents are "pretty good guys."

The big problem in Lisa's life right now is her feelings for James, a quiet but kind of rebellious senior at her school. He was suspended once last year for a minor drug possession, but Lisa knows that he's really a wonderful guy with an awful home situation. She made the mistake of telling her folks about him a couple months ago, and her dad came down pretty hard on her. He said she was too young to be dating a senior, much less one who's been in trouble with drugs. So Lisa hasn't told her folks about her after-school walks in the park with James, where they just spend time talking. When she comes home late in the afternoon, she says that she's been over at Laurie's, who will cover for her if necessary. Lisa's plan is just to play it cool for a while, until she finds a good way to introduce James to her parents so they can see he's all right.

But now something unexpected has come up. James is going on a ski trip with some friends from Greg's college—in fact, Greg knows them and he'll probably join the group for part of the weekend. James invited Lisa along and asked her if she could work it out with her parents. She told James it would be no problem, especially with her brother there—but she knew she couldn't tell her folks the whole truth.

So when she approached her parents, she told them it would be a trip organized by teachers from her high school, not James's and Greg's college friends. It was a lie, but just a little one. She thought it would spare her parents unnecessary worry—and not incidentally, it would guarantee their permission for the trip. After all, it wasn't like she would be in danger. There would be older girls there, and she knows she can take care of herself anyway.

Still, the whole thing has made Lisa pretty nervous and she's only mentioned it once to her folks, over two weeks ago. Now it's dinnertime on Wednesday night, and she's leaving with James from school on Friday afternoon for the trip. She has to say something now. . . .

LISA: Um, Mom, you know that ski trip I told you about?

PEG: Ski trip? What trip was that, honey?

LISA: You know, the one I told you about last week. The one to Silver Valley.

GENE: Silver Valley? That's in the mountains up by Greg's campus, isn't it?

LISA: Yeah, that's right. Remember I told you that Greg

would be there, too? He's going to meet our, uh, group from school.

PEG: Oh, that'll be nice. When is this happening, honey?

LISA: This weekend, Mom. We'll be going up Friday afternoon.

PEG: [*Putting down her fork*] Friday afternoon? Lisa, that's two days from now! You don't have anything ready.

LISA: Yes, I do, Mom. It's not a big deal; I'm just going for the weekend.

PEG: How many of your friends from school are going?

LISA: Oh, I don't know. . . . There'll be ten or twelve people staying in the lodge. Greg will be there, and maybe some friends of his.

GENE: Well, it sounds like fun. Do you have to ride all the way up there in a bus, or what?

LISA: Uh, no . . . I'm gonna ride up in a car.

PEG: [*Looking worriedly at Gene*] You mean you're all going up in several cars? Who's going to be driving you, honey?

LISA: [*Shifting in her chair*] Well, just one of the older guys, I guess.

PEG: Wait a minute, honey. Isn't this trip being chaperoned by some teachers? Why aren't they driving?

LISA: Oh, Mom, don't worry about it. I'll be okay. I told you Greg would be there—

GENE: I don't think you answered your mother's question, Lisa. Where are your teachers going to be? What kind of trip is this exactly?

LISA: [*Whining*] Dad, you don't have to make a big *investigation* out of it! Look . . . it was actually James who invited me. We talk at school sometimes, you know, and when he found out that some of his friends know Greg, he thought it would be fun if—

GENE: This is the boy with the drugs?

LISA: No! I mean, that was only one time. He doesn't do that stuff anymore. He's really okay, Dad. He's nice and you'd both really like him if you gave him a chance!

GENE: Well, you can just forget about that, miss. You've been lying to us about this trip, and that blows any chances you *or* this James could have with me. We try to give you a pretty loose rein, Lisa, but I won't put up with being lied to.

[*To Peg*] I think we'd better ground this little girl for a while, don't you?

PEG: Well, Gene, let's not be too harsh. I think we all need to talk things over, but obviously this trip is out of the question.

LISA: [*Crying*] I am *not* a little girl, Daddy! Why don't you trust me? Have I ever been bad?

GENE: That's not the point, Lisa. Making up a story like this is bad enough for me. You can just forget about making any big trips *or* staying out after school until you're ready to tell the truth. Is that clear?

[*Lisa stares angrily at her father without replying.*]

GENE: Lisa, I asked you: Is—that—clear?

LISA: [*Biting her lip*] Maybe I'll just go anyway. You can't stop me.

PEG: Lisa! What on earth are you saying?

LISA: [*Increasingly defiant*] I'm saying maybe I just won't be here for dinner Friday. We can leave from school and you can't do anything about it.

GENE: Like hell we can't—

PEG: Gene!

[*Lisa runs from the table, sobbing, and Peg and Gene stare at each other in exasperation.*]

One of the toughest challenges faced by parents is the negotiation of their children's growing independence, and it's made even tougher when parents do not have open, supportive communications between themselves. In Chapter 9 you'll see how Gene becomes alert to his upset feelings early enough in this family scene to ask his wife to pursue Ethical Persuasion for the benefit of everyone involved. Although the specific outcome of the conflict will be similar, the difference in mutual respect and understanding will be dramatic.

It's easy to see how each of the preceding conversations went awry at the point when strong feelings erupted for one or more of the participants. Many communication strategies suggest that feelings must be pacified or put aside before constructive negotiations can proceed. In reality, that's impossible—because our feelings arise from the deepest, most creative and spontaneous part of ourselves. We need to learn how to recognize, respect, and hear feelings out fully *before* constructive solutions can be devised. Allowing everyone in a sensitive negotiation to state their feelings and opinions fully—in an atmosphere of respect, understanding, caring, and fairness—is the heart of Ethical Persuasion.

2

Feelings Are Facts

S cience, technology, and finance dominate the cultures and thinking of the industrialized world. In these fields, a great deal of effort is made to minimize or even eliminate the effects of feelings, which are seen as irrational, unpredictable, too "feminine," and downright dangerous. In business, strong feelings are regarded as unprofessional, something that should be expressed only at home or in intimate relationships. Hardly anyone explores and shares their feelings as part of the process of professional decision making—or if they do, they're not likely to admit it to co-workers, superiors, or subordinates.

Yet the key to all kinds of relationships is how feelings are experienced, managed, and communicated. *Relationships are based on feelings,* even when feelings seem so far in the background as to be nonexistent. For instance, even calling a distant, anonymous operator to order a product from a catalog will go better if the operator sounds friendly. If he or she is brusque or cold, our impression of the company, and any later dealings with it, will tend to be influenced negatively by the feelings we had in re-action to that treatment. First impressions are largely based on feelings.

Communication breaks down dramatically whenever strong feelings, good or bad, get in the way. How many conflicts have you experienced that were due purely to misinformation, "crossed lines," or confusion with no sig-nificant emotional overtones? How severe or lasting were such simple misunderstandings compared to conflicts in which strong feelings played a role?

"Stop Being So Emotional!"

While conducting an Ethical Persuasion workshop for frontline managers in a large retail corporation, I heard a classic tale of emotional eruption and denial in professional communications. The story was related by Terry, a veteran store manager who was unusually honest and open with both her supervisors and subordinates. Her personal style had always gone against the grain of behind-the-back hy-pocrisy and authoritarian manipulation that were rampant in the company as a whole.

About a month before a meeting requested by Frank Johnson, the corporate vice president of operations, Terry and her fellow managers had received a memo from the head office about new cost-cutting standards for all the stores. The memo sent a shock wave through the ranks of managers: the company was demanding the maintenance of high service standards while forcing managers to lay off employees in order to lower costs. To the managers it looked like a no-win situation. Already lean on staff, they were almost certain to fall below the cost or quality standards. Either way it would cost them their quarterly bonuses, a significant part of their income.

By the time of Frank's check-in visit to the region, Terry had been unofficially appointed by her peers to air their grievances. A ten-year company veteran with an excellent track record, she could not be dismissed easily by headquarters.

At a lunch meeting after the salad and the small talk were finished, Frank gave Terry one of his most paternal smiles and said, "Okay, Terry, you're the one I always depend on to cut through the bull and tell me what's really going on. So how are things on the front line?"

Tense and unsmiling, Terry responded, "You want the truth, Mr. Johnson?"

"Of course!" he said, raising both his palms toward the ceiling and smiling even more broadly. "Hit me with your best shot."

"Well," said Terry, pausing a moment to take a breath before plunging in, "it looks like you guys have done it again. You just laid these new cost standards on us without the least bit of consultation out here in the field. It was a done deal before we knew what hit us, and everyone I've talked to agrees that there's more to this than meets the eye. You know we can't maintain the kind of service standards you're famous for demanding and lower costs at the same time! If we fail, there go our bonuses! And I think —we all think—that's part of the overall *strategy*, Mr. Johnson. You're not just cutting frontline labor costs. You're cutting managers' pay, too, only you're doing it in the most backhanded way imaginable. You're going to make us fail, and then say, 'You people can't expect bonuses if you can't meet the standards!' "

By now Terry's voice had risen to the high pitch she always tried to avoid, because she knew it meant she was close to tears. She certainly didn't need her mascara running down her cheeks and her credibility going down the drain in a meeting with a corporate VP. Trying to calm herself, Terry deliberately lowered her voice and finished her speech more slowly: "*That's* what's going on at the front lines, Mr. Johnson. You've got a lot of ticked-off managers."

By now the vice president's smile had faded to a tense, narrow line across his face. Terry could see his neck flushing red as a few uncomfortable moments of silence passed between them. Frank was known for alternating between soft-spoken fatherliness and angry explosions—the latter often coming soon after he had invited someone to "hit me with your best shot"—and Terry knew she had really asked for it this time. But as she plaintively asked me later during the workshop, what else could she have done? Frank simply had to face "the truth."

"That's *ridiculous!*" Frank had thundered in reply. "What a bunch of crybabies you people are! That cost decision was made purely on an accounting basis, Terry. You know damn well that we've been changing the mix of products coming off the line, and that should require progressively less labor up front. You people know that! But you're reacting like a bunch of spoiled-rotten kids, ignoring any facts that don't happen to fit your little conspiracy theory."

Frank leaned forward suddenly, giving Terry a little scare, and poked aggressively at his own chest with one thumb. "But that's why I'm here, Terry. *I* have to deal with *all* the facts, and I try to deal with *just* the facts. So let's stop being so emotional for a minute, okay? You're just running wild with this paranoid idea that everybody upstairs is some kind of penny-pinching ogre who doesn't care about people having to make a living. You're being incredibly unfair, Terry, and you know it. You're one of our most seasoned people out here, and I expect more from you than this kind of immature rookie-manager bitching. Let me tell you, we aren't allowed to be so childish and irrational in upper management, Terry." Leaning back, Frank straightened his tie and shifted his gaze abruptly from Terry to the window.

Reciting Frank's outburst to me at the workshop, Terry remembered wondering whether he had deliberately intended to make a point about her promotion potential. "But I didn't really care about that," she related. "All I cared about was that I had gotten exactly nowhere, and nowhere is where the rest of that conversation went. That's the problem with telling the truth to our executives, Tom," Terry said with a sigh. "It just blows up in our faces."

Reviewing the Barriers

Trying to troubleshoot this confrontation for Terry and her manager peers, I pointed out that all five of the fundamental barriers to communication (see page 9) had been present in this conversation. "One: Terry, you and Frank Johnson obviously live in unique and private worlds—not just as individuals, but also as an executive and a manager. It's plain to see that each of you has suspicion about the other's world. Most of you frontline managers tend to think corporate executives are up to no good, and Frank shows *his* bias with that crack about 'rookie-manager bitching.'

"Two: I think it's safe to say that both of you felt a natural and understandable insecurity. Terry, you know that you weren't exactly looking forward to telling Frank the truth as you saw it"—at this Terry nodded her head vigorously—"and I think you can all imagine that Frank probably says things like 'hit me with your best shot' to cover up his anxiety. He wants to look both strong and upbeat when he knows something's about to hit the fan. But he's just as insecure as any human being—assuming, that is, that corporate managers *are* human beings." The embarrassed laughter following this remark let me know that at least a few people in the audience acknowledged their resentful, defensive mindset.

"Three: Neither you nor Frank was able to handle the strong feelings that came up for each of you. You, Terry, said you were about to cry, which you thought would make you look weak. Frank just blew up emotionally, all the while telling you to stop being so emotional! This is right in line with traditional masculine rules for communication at work: only the boss can get angry, and no one must ever cry.

"This leads directly to the fourth classic obstacle: Frank was not only denying the fact that he was having strong feelings, but he also wanted you, Terry, to deny that feelings were a legitimate part of your experience. Notice that I'm not talking about whether anybody's feelings were *right* or *wrong*—just that they were there, very powerful, and therefore carried important messages. Frank tried openly to stop Terry's feelings, which felt to her like a complete rejection of everything she had to say. And Terry, you'll have to admit that you ended up rejecting

Frank—because you reacted to his *display of feelings,* just as much as anything he said, by deciding the situation was hopeless."

Terry nodded very slowly, perhaps not entirely conceding my point. "Finally," I continued, "the power imbalance between you two is as plain as can be, but there was no respectful discussion of it. Frank may or may not have been using his superior position to threaten Terry professionally. But neither of them was admitting the relative *vulnerability* of their respective positions. Believe me, there's just as much vulnerability when you're on top as when you're down below. Everybody answers to someone, and no one is safe. Everyone feels like their position is on the line."

Feelings as a Bridge

After a coffee break, I tried to introduce Terry and the other managers to a different perception of the feelings that can seem so problematic we are tempted to ignore them or shut them down. "If you get nothing else from this seminar," I went on, "I hope you begin to look at feelings in a new way. Not as uncontrollable, dangerous energies that can screw up your most important communications, but as the very *bridge* that forms and keeps a relationship going. Feelings come from the deepest part of ourselves and give us our spiritual connection. Managed well, feelings are the medium of caring and influence between people. Managed poorly, strong feelings become the explosives that can destroy relationships.

"But feelings are something else, too: they are information about oneself and others, messages about who you are, what you need and care about, what's right and wrong for you, what you have to share with each other. So feelings are both the *process* and most of the *content* of relationships. And process is more important than content here. If your feelings aren't connecting you to each other, then the messages of your feelings aren't going to get through by any other means—"

Terry interrupted my spiel. "I can understand feelings as a bridge between myself and someone else when the feelings are good. But how do you keep bad feelings from blowing up the bridge? Doesn't having a lot of bad feelings tell you that the relationship just isn't working?"

"Well," I conceded, "in your conversation with Frank the bad feelings you both had were certainly signals that *something* was going wrong. But there's a way to use those uncomfortable signals in a positive way—that is, to see that *upset feelings give you an opportunity to deepen a relationship*. If you get in the habit of avoiding any upset feelings in order to keep everything smooth, then you're going to have a lot of superficial relationships at best. The key to getting the most out of strong feelings in a relationship, whether they're good or bad feelings, is to handle them all with caring and respect."

I paused, feeling the difficulty of analyzing a vast web of connections. "But I'm getting a little ahead of myself. First we need to back up and look at where feelings, as the most intimate facts of our experience and our identity, come from."

Feelings Come First

For the next hour I gave the managers my view on the origin and purpose of feelings, a view I've drawn from my studies and practical experience as a self-change guide. With its emphasis on logic, rationality, and objective perception, science has long dismissed feelings as a purely subjective realm inappropriate for investigation. But recent research into brain functioning suggests that human beings experience a great deal of sensation and feeling in infancy, well before our rational thinking processes have come into play. The effects on our identity and sense of self are enormous.

As explained in a June 24, 1991, article by science writer Margie Patlak in the *Los Angeles Times:*

> Much of the recent research on emotions centers on the amygdala, a small, almond-shaped brain structure. The amygdala acts as both a gateway to emotions and a filter for memory by attaching significance to the vast array of information that is sent to the brain by the senses. . . . [Thus] emotions not only shape what we perceive but what we remember.
>
> "Emotions really influence what you get out of the world . . ." [said National Institute of Mental Health neuroscientist Mortimer Mishkin]. Although most people are unaware of it, emotions guide our behavior by drawing us toward something favorable and propelling us from something harmful, according to New York University neuroscientist Joseph LeDoux. . . .
>
> In babies, the parts of the [thinking] cortex that can counter an emotional reaction do not operate fully until . . . several months after the amygdala and other emotional centers in the brain become active. Researchers believe much emotional information is recorded permanently by the amygdala before it can be overridden by the cortex.
>
> "The amygdala doesn't seem to have an eraser. . . . From a very early age, we build emotional records that subsequently will influence everything we do," said LeDoux.

This is neurological confirmation of what psychologists and therapists have long known: the intense feeling experiences of infancy and childhood strongly influence our behavior and our sense of self for the rest of our lives. If our earliest experiences are less than ideal, then we're going to have at least a few powerfully negative feeling patterns—and most of us will have many—that become part of our basic identity.

Feelings, Spirit, and Self-Concept

If we could perceive and analyze bad feelings rationally at a tender age, we would know that those feelings meant something was going wrong in our environment: maybe Mother or Father weren't giving us enough loving attention, or perhaps were actively abusing us. But children do not clearly differentiate themselves from their family and their environment until they are several years of age, and thus they make an understandable but erroneous conclusion: if things happen that make me *feel* bad, I must *be* bad. Feelings seem to arise from the deepest parts of ourselves (we feel things in our "heart," "bones," and "guts"), and at an early age it's thus impossible to separate our bad feelings from our very essence. For many years, children who don't receive sufficient comforting misinterpret deeply felt, painful emotions as evidence of something wrong deep inside themselves.

Unfortunately, most people never grow out of this mind trap. We continue to believe that bad feelings are evidence of our badness, rather than signals that something unhealthy is happening to us (whether it's done to us by others or ourselves). Thus, we have a strong motivation to avoid or push back bad feelings; after all, no one likes to feel defective. Another motivation for avoiding negative feelings arises as we grow up and are consistently taught that our thinking functions are superior to our feeling functions. Instead of learning to *interpret* our feelings with the help of our rational capacities, we learn to dismiss or denigrate feelings. (Did you notice how the writer of the *Times* article assumed that the function of rational thinking is to "counter" or "override" emotions? The bias is everywhere!)

Yet as even neuroscientists admit, we feel feelings before we think thoughts, and they help create the core of our identity, our fundamental sense of worth as human beings. Feelings cannot be long ignored without erupting in erratic, disguised, and dangerous ways—as aggression, compulsive behavior, or even disease. In fact, by the time most of us become aware of intense negative feelings, they have been building and becoming distorted inside us for a while. Thus, they tend to arise in a sort of code that requires some patience and deliberate practice to decipher.

Feelings arise ceaselessly from the deepest part of ourselves, what I call our "inner spirit." That spirit expresses our particular combination of talents, vulnerabilities, resilience, compassion, and neediness. The more we respect, listen to, and learn to interpret our feelings, both good and bad, the more spirited and natural our personalities will be. The more we suppress or dismiss our feelings, the more our personality will tend to be cold, phony, and dispirited. Of course, the irresponsible acting-out of raw feelings creates chaos and can get us arrested, hospitalized, or killed.

Somewhere between spirit and personality arises *self-concept,* the fundamental idea about who we are. Because negative feeling experiences from childhood are imprinted on everyone, most people have a significant amount of self-doubt within their self-concept. It is simply the human condition to feel some loss, rejection, failure, and deprivation at our very core, because we all experienced these feelings from the moment of our birth.

The Familiarity Principle

At this point, one might reasonably ask why we don't naturally learn to do everything in our power to improve our self-concept as we mature and become independent of our earliest influences. To some extent, most of us do improve our self-concept—or at least we construct an outer personality that *looks* confident and self-assured. But the temptation to continue using bad feelings as evidence of the unworthiness we feel inside is supported by a very powerful mechanism in the human psyche, which I call the familiarity principle:

> *You cannot act or be treated in ways that are different from those you are used to—even if those ways are better—without becoming increasingly uncomfortable.*

In terms of physical survival, familiarity usually equals safety, for both animals and humans. But human beings extend this equation to their psychological reality, particularly in terms of self-concept. Thus, if someone grows up with a lot of self-doubt, almost no amount of positive, rewarding experiences and feelings will substantially alter her poor self-concept . . . *unless she decides to deliberately change the way she looks at herself, her experiences, and her feelings.* This will require concrete changes in her attitudes and actions as well.

Changing oneself in this way is tremendously difficult, which is why most people resist doing it until their familiar way of life has become so uncomfortable, unrewarding, or dangerous that venturing into unfamiliar realms seems worth the risk. For instance, most alcoholics have to "bottom out"—or be dramatically confronted by friends and relatives in carefully orchestrated interventions—before they turn to a therapist or recovery program for help.

As a psychological counselor, I focus on helping individuals undertake the difficult process of self-change. I act as a guide, a coach, and a cheerleader for people who are preparing to change their personalities and their inner self-concept in positive directions. I help them get in touch with their inner spirit—the only reliable, lifelong guide for personal growth—by teaching them how to listen to and interpret all their feelings as messages about which directions to go in life. I try to help them balance their thinking and feeling functions. And I explore with them the fundamental values of respect, understanding, caring, and fairness, values which help anchor us to our inner spirit. (More about this in Chapter 3.)

Ethical Persuasion is the interpersonal application of the counseling mode I call "guided self-change." Thus, EP isn't just a negotiation strategy, but also a method of healing self-doubt and alienation within oneself. If you learn to respect and appreciate another's feelings, you will learn to treat your own feelings more wisely in the process. That can be your way out of a lot of the inherent confusion and pain of the human condition. I hoped I could convey at least a little of the tremendous potential of EP to Terry and her peers after explaining this much. First, I had to see if they were ready to look at their problematic supervisor in a new light.

Seeing the Hurt Behind All Anger

"If you accept that we all carry imprints of hurt and loss from our earliest years," I began, "and that those wounds still influence our self-concept, then you can begin to perceive the deep background of all human conflict. It's absolutely true that strong feelings can get in the way of rational decision making, because they stir up our personal bias. That bias is always attached to our earliest experiences of pain, as well as to later significant traumas. Either way, we react defensively against *feeling inadequate,* no matter what we might *say* we're angry about. We're a lot less likely simply to admit that something is hurting us or making us uncomfortable than we are to withdraw or get angry and go on the attack. Are you with me so far?"

Most of the people in the room nodded. Terry, never one to let things go by unchallenged, spoke up. "I think I see where you're going, Tom. But when Frank got angry, I couldn't worry about his childhood pain or his self-doubt. I had to be looking out for our interests, not psychoanalyzing the boss, for goodness' sake!"

"Fair enough," I said, laughing. "I'm certainly the last person to say that *anybody* needs to be psychoanalyzed. The only thing you have to remember for the purposes of learning Ethical Persuasion is that hurt, whether it's rooted in the past or happening right in the moment, lies behind all anger. Let's look at your side of things, Terry. What did Frank say that hurt your feelings?"

"Almost everything," she replied. "He called us all immature—and not for the first time, by the way—and he completely dismissed our legitimate fear about our bonuses. He really didn't listen to me at all."

"Can you see that hurt is the core of your anger, then?"

"No problem."

"Okay," I ventured, "can you imagine how Frank might have been hurt by anything you said?"

Turning the tables slowed Terry down for a moment. "Well," she murmured thoughtfully, "he did say that it sounds like we're accusing him of caring only about money. And he seemed a little overwhelmed, I guess—I can imagine he's under a lot of pressure from upstairs *and* downstairs. But that's his job, isn't it? And he's making a hell of a lot more than I am, that's for sure. I can't be responsible for his feelings being hurt because he has a tough job!"

"You don't have to be," I reassured her. "You only need to be *aware* that his feelings are hurt, and so are yours, and that you're both sensitive, vulnerable human beings. Negotiations are pretty impossible when you have two people talking who each have their own bad feelings/self-doubt cycle going full tilt and are extremely defensive as a result. When anything that person A says evokes bad feelings in person B, then B is going to doubt his own worth, blame himself for having bad feelings, *and* blame A for being the cause of his pain. Pretty soon, the subject of the discussion is just being used as a weapon in a battle over hurt and angry feelings. For instance, the issue of cost allowances rapidly became secondary between you and Frank.

"So the signal for shifting into Ethical Persuasion is whenever you become aware of strong feelings rising up in yourself or in the other person. That's when you make a special effort to *acknowledge* the presence and power of feelings, rather than push them back or use their energy to defend yourself or mount an attack."

"I don't know, Tom," Terry said skeptically. "It sounds good if you're a person who's incredibly alert to everybody's feelings. But my own feelings always get away from me before I know what's happening. What good is EP after the damage is done?"

"Lots of good!" I exclaimed. "Let's take that moment when Frank turned away from you after his outburst. You said that you really didn't get anywhere after that point, right?"

"Absolutely nowhere. We batted around the same things we'd already said and then we were just icy and silent through most of lunch. Then I ordered a big dessert on his tab and had to take an antacid when I got back to work."

A wave of laughter rose from Terry's co-workers.

"Well," I replied, "you can certainly see that your feelings kept running the show, whether or not it was good for you. Let's back up to that moment after Frank's big blow-up, and imagine that your next reply to him went something like this:

Well, Mr. Johnson, I know that I *can* get pretty irrational when I'm upset. But look, all we can do at our level is react to what's coming down on us from upstairs. Maybe we really don't understand the situation and we're missing the whole point. But our feelings start with how this situation looks to us. What else do we have to go by? It looks like it's really going to hurt our take-home pay. I'm not saying we're totally in the right, but I do have to say this is how we feel, even if it seems unfair to you. And I think it's important for you folks in senior management to know exactly how we feel, Mr. Johnson.

"Do you think this kind of explanation might have smoothed things out a little bit, Terry?" I inquired.

"Maybe," she conceded.

"All right. But we're not really into Ethical Persuasion yet. To take the first step of EP—which would give you a tremendous strategic advantage, by the way—you could have said something like this instead:

> Okay, Mr. Johnson, I guess it's clear that we're both pretty upset. I've said that store managers are worried that the new cost standards are going to affect our bonuses. You may be right that we're not looking at the whole story, but I guess I need to hear more about that in detail. We really need to know how you arrived at this decision, because so far we only feel the results. Since we *are* very upset about the new standards, can you help me understand exactly why and how they came about? I really want to understand your view of the facts as thoroughly as I can, so that I have new information to take back to the others.

"The point of this approach," I explained, "is to give both sides some emotional breathing room. You're not denying your feelings, but you're not going to let them run the whole show, either. You're inviting the other person to use the energy of his feelings to state his whole case. Later on, that courtesy should give you a better chance at having your side heard thoroughly, plus it will give you some leverage when you get to negotiations—much more so than if you kept battling it out. You're not giving in; you're actually directing the situation by keeping the lines of communication open. To be the one who initiates that positive action gives you tremendous personal power, regardless of your position in the company."

Terry nodded thoughtfully and everyone in the room seemed to have more than enough to think about until another session. But I had hardly touched on another building block of Ethical Persuasion: the recognition and endorsement of *respect, understanding, caring,* and *fairness* as fundamental values for human communication. Feelings are facts of our experience, but even when balanced with our rational functions, they are not sufficient to guide our actions and negotiations in a consistently positive and healthy direction. We need the power of values to contact the wisdom and immeasurable creativity of the human spirit.

3

The Power of Values

What does the word *power* mean to you? If you lend an ear to advertising and everyday conversations, you'll probably hear the word used most often in two ways: as what it takes to get a car from zero to sixty in a few seconds, and as the capacity of someone to control or affect other people. Thus, it can be said that power has two principal meanings in popular usage: *the energy to get things done* and *the ability to influence people*.

For the purposes of learning Ethical Persuasion, I'd like you to consider a new definition of power:

Power is creative influence.

By creative influence, I mean the ability to affect any human interaction in a way that *adds energy* to the situation, and in a way that leads to results which are greater than the sum of their parts.

Not every conversation needs a lot of creative influence to succeed, but crucial conversations always do. Crucial conversations are those in which strong feelings arise at some point, usually because the stakes are high in one way or another. If the raw energy of strong feelings is not managed intelligently, then it can rapidly drain meaning away from the conversation or be painfully neutralized as it conflicts with the energy of feelings expressed by others (or even with contrary feelings one may be experiencing within oneself).

Ethical Persuasion enables you to develop the ability to creatively influence any kind of high-stakes negotiations, whether personal or official, intimate or business oriented. It gives you the power to cultivate cooperation in all your important exchanges, with or without the initial friendliness of the other side of any exchange. Cultivating cooperation in all kinds of situations requires learning to manage intelligently the raw energy of our feelings and thoughts.

This energy is the ceaselessly arising gift of our human spirit, but it must be guided effectively to be of any use to us as creative influence. In this chapter we'll discuss how to use four fundamental values of communication—*respect, understanding, caring,* and *fairness*—as the guidelines for learning how to transform raw spiritual energy into personal power.

First, let's look at how that kind of personal power differs from the kind we've resented, resisted, and fought for all our lives.

Personal Power and
Positional Power

Imagine two high school science teachers in a well-integrated urban school system. We'll call them Nick Carson and Angela Perez. Working on opposite sides of the district, they face common problems of dwindling funds, inadequate facilities, and an increasing population of troubled, disruptive students. Both spend more time on crowd control and bureaucratic paper shuffling than they would like, and both have serious concerns about the future of the public schools. But there are some remarkable differences between their results. For three years in a row, Angela Perez's science classes have won awards in statewide science fairs, and her students' grades are higher than the system's average overall. Nick Carson's students seldom manage to put together any science fair project whatsoever, and the truancy rate for his classes is the only thing about them that's above average.

To his students, Mr. Carson is an ogre—a harsh, screeching disciplinarian who makes it clear that he demands respect while he really gets only temporary, superficial obedience and sniggering, behind-his-back ridicule. By contrast, most of Mrs. Perez's students regard her as a special kind of friend—someone older and truly wiser who gets and keeps their attention just by being herself. Some of the students even confide their personal problems to her, although none of the kids would mistake her for "just one of the gang." She keeps her distance as a teacher; it just seems that anyone can cross that distance when they need to and ask her for help about an assignment or almost anything else.

Both of these teachers have *positional power*, the ability

to influence their students in the way that's prescribed by their job descriptions. But only one of them has significant *personal power,* the creative kind of influence that not only magnifies her positional authority, but increases the respectful response and productive output of her students as well. An observer of the two teachers might conclude that Angela Perez is simply a "better person" by her very nature.

In fact, she only *understands* herself and the students better than Nick Carson. She *respects* her students as full-fledged human beings just like herself, if younger and less experienced, and she respects her own ability to educate —that is, to draw out from her students their true potential. She *cares* about their needs and vulnerabilities just as she cares about her own, and does her best to be *fair* to everyone in a difficult, demanding environment. This means being fair to herself as a limited and needy individual, who makes sure to find advice, comfort, and support from her peers and family.

Nick Carson suffers from a lack of personal power because his self-doubt prevents him from activating those four fundamental values in his own life or in his exchanges with students. He fears his own nature—fears, in fact, that he would become a puppet of his students if he let his real caring for them show. So he reacts against his fear by putting on the act of a tyrant. With his fellow teachers he denigrates the young people in his charge, and never lets on that the challenges of teaching provoke in him any more than a bitter, sardonic laugh over the futility of it all. In fact, he feels deeply hurt a hundred times a day, and he covers that hurt with an all-purpose anger.

Can Nick Carson change and become a better teacher? Absolutely. But he will have to risk new ways of communicating with his students, peers, friends, and family—ways of communicating that will frighten him and make him feel like he's sailing right into the unknown. That's exactly where he will be sailing: into the unknown parts of himself, his inborn energetic capacities that have gone long undeveloped. Those capacities will further lead him into the unfamiliar arena of healthier relationships.

To start the journey, Nick will first have to decide that respect, understanding, caring, and fairness are values worth pursuing in his personal life and career. He will have to concede that his current way of being is proof that he knows very little about those values or his own spirit. And then he will have to decide that he's willing to learn. At that point, Nick Carson could undertake Ethical Persuasion not only to improve his teaching, but to improve his understanding of himself as well. That won't immediately ease the difficulties he faces as a public school teacher. But it will increasingly give him a taste of the real power and happiness that Angela Perez finds in her work every day.

The Birthplace of Positional Power

In a very real sense, everyone is born under the thumb of positional power. It is simply the human condition to arrive in the world helpless and utterly without power (except the first power to cry out and make one's needs known). And every parent is an instant boss, whether she or he has ever experienced any other positional authority up to that point in life. From the moment of birth, the entire responsibility for the health and welfare of another human being rests with the parents—a responsibility they will feel, to some degree, for the rest of their lives.

The gradual transfer of responsibility from parents to the child occasions one negotiation of power after another, particularly in the child's adolescent years. Whether those negotiations will be power struggles or carefully managed mutual experiments depends largely on the parents' capacity for mature, creative influence. The effects of those negotiations on a child will be lifelong, for he or she will always tend to relate to authority, resist authority, and assume authority in patterns that repeat or rebel against the patterns of power in the family of origin.

It's valuable to remember this fact when entering into any kind of sensitive negotiations, for it can explain much of the bizarre, irrational, and impulsive responses that may crop up in you or in another person when feelings become intense. We can't take responsibility for someone else's childhood difficulties just because they may be the root of feelings that are complicating an adult exchange. But we can make an effort to keep in mind the *human condition* of being born into powerlessness, and having our earliest emotional wounds imprinted onto our fundamental sense of self. We all live in unique and private worlds, but often what we are fiercely hiding in those worlds is our private struggle with the mistaken idea that we are not "good enough" to be loved, respected, and treated fairly.

Simply remembering that we share this common struggle as individuals will not magically create a utopian community in which no one exerts positional power. In fact, positional power is not a problem in itself; it's a necessary tool for social organization. Problems arise only when we rely on or defer to positional power at the expense of our personal power in our relationships. That happens whenever any one of us wholly identifies himself or herself as a teacher, parent, manager, executive, subordinate, or a "nobody"—instead of as a unique and inherently worthy human being serving a particular function in a family, organization, or society.

Personal Power Is Permanent

Our positions in society will probably change quite a bit during our life span, and our positional power will go up and down with those changes. But personal power—one's individual brand of creative influence—is permanent and can only be enhanced once its nature is truly understood and affirmed. It is our spiritual fingerprint, and it can leave a lasting impression long after our physical death.

You can have or attain positional power without exercising respect, understanding, caring, and fairness. We have plenty of managers, teachers, ministers, and politicians who are evidence of that. But genuine personal power is impossible without the four bedrock values of relationship. By endorsing, exploring, and integrating them into your daily life, you can eventually develop tremendous personal power.

The effect of great personal power on positional power is somewhat paradoxical; the first kind can eventually make the second kind almost irrelevant. I have known corporate executives with so much personal power that they haven't given a directive to their subordinates in years, because there's no need for them to do so. They feel free to go to subordinates, ask "What do you think about such-and-such?", discuss the matter fairly and completely, and arrive at a resolution together. In the process it may be forgotten who originated the final solution, and the subordinates often end up with a lot of the credit. The effect on these value-driven executives? *Their personal power keeps increas-*

ing as they develop reputations for having "mysterious" abilities to get their employees to outdo themselves.

The same can be true of parenting, a realm where teaching by example is infinitely more powerful than ruling by positional authority. The recent vogue of "Just Say No" campaigns to reduce the usage of drugs by schoolchildren reminds me of a brief exchange I had with my older son, Scott, when he was a senior in high school. My wife, Judy, and I had begun to worry that he was becoming a homebody and a loner, spending nearly every weekend at home studying and watching TV, turning down many invitations to last-semester parties from his classmates. We always tried to let our kids know our honest concerns and feelings when they came up, instead of automatically telling them what to do. So I knocked on Scott's door one sunny Saturday morning and said, "Hey, Scott, what are you up to this weekend?"

Opening the door, Scott looked at me curiously and as I entered he returned to his desk. "Oh, I just wanted to stay home and catch some football games on TV and try to get some reading done. You want to shoot some baskets later, Dad?"

"Sure," I replied. Not sure of how to say what was on my mind, I continued awkwardly: "Look, your mom and I are worried that maybe you're not having much fun these days. You never go to those parties that you get invited to."

Scott gave me his best what-in-the-world-is-this-about look and then said, "Dad, please. I'm on the football team and the wrestling team, and I do lots of things with my friends after school during the week. But I have an A-minus average and I want to keep it that way. The problem with the parties I've been to is that kids are smoking grass and drinking a lot. Some of them are even doing heavier stuff. That's what they call having fun, but it's just not exciting to me. If I wanted to drink, I know you'd let me have something out of the cabinet, and you'd probably let me smoke pot here if I asked. But really, that stuff is pretty boring."

I was so surprised to be getting a lecture about the drudgery of drugs and drink that for once I didn't have an answer at the ready. Scott filled in: "If it's really upsetting you and Mom, I'll go to a couple parties and stay awhile, but what's the point? If you want to know the truth, I'm looking forward to college where I might find some friends more like myself."

In fact, Scott went on to be elected president of his college fraternity and his medical school's student body. He never did develop a taste for mood-altering substances. Was he a miracle child, and Judy and myself perfect parents? Not by a long shot. But we have always worked to keep the lines of honest communication open to our children, respecting the immense capacity of their inborn spirits to guide their growth more profoundly and effectively than our parental authority ever could by itself. Besides, we knew we didn't have all the answers even for ourselves!

For parents, the beauty of exemplifying and relying on the values of healthy relating is that when kids run into unanticipated situations in which an authority is not present, they can rely on their own internal values to make consistent, healthy choices aligned with their spirit. "Just Say No" is not a deeply rooted, affirmative value. It depends entirely on the persuasiveness of authority figures, celebrities, and pressure from peers—the kinds of influence which can be easily forgotten or overwhelmed in stressful situations. When kids are facing situations that their parents never faced in their lives (which will happen to every generation, to some extent), they are best guided by self-respect, understanding of their real needs, a sense of caring for themselves and others, and fairness.

Parents can do nothing better for their children than help them maximize their personal, permanent power by modeling it. Hardly any family is in such bad shape that it cannot give Ethical Persuasion a try as a route to regaining everyone's internal sense of direction and reconnecting with each other. (For specific applications of EP to family politics, see Chapter 9.)

Defining the Values

You may have noticed that I've been talking about the application of respect, understanding, caring, and fairness to communications without having yet explicitly defined these four values. I'm not going to do that anywhere in this book. There are two somewhat contradictory reasons for not defining the values in detail. First, each of us has a pretty good notion of what these ideals mean. Second, most of us have only begun to experience their meaning deeply. In other words, these are *experiential values* whose meanings deepen and expand with exploration—and whose power is as inexhaustible as the spirit they connect us with. I could never define for you all that these values can mean in your own experience, and we might never agree on a precise definition for each. I can, however, point the way toward your own exploration of what it means to be respectful, understanding, caring, and fair to yourself and everyone you encounter.

I do feel that it's necessary to distinguish the four values I am espousing from the kind of "moral values" that some politicians and religious leaders have recently urged us to "return" to in order to heal some of our most serious societal ills. The problem with values such as "family devotion," "sexual morality," and "social order" is that they refer to certain *codes of conduct* that cannot be applied fairly to all kinds of people in all situations, however well-intended such codes may seem to their proponents. In a democratic and heterogeneous society such as ours, we will never be able to impose universal codes of conduct by legislation or moral exhortation. But we can all begin to improve our individual ways of relating—out of which the fabric of societal conduct is surely woven—by resolving to explore and exemplify respect, understanding, caring, and fairness. These are open-ended values of relationship which I believe *can* be universally endorsed.

Why? Because these values at least begin to describe the conditions required for the health and vitality of the universal human spirit. I often suggest to people in counseling and workshops that these values help to anchor our feelings to our shared spirit. Feelings arise from a primary, energetic, and spiritual level, but they can become distorted as they come up through the unconscious and conscious layers of personality and are put to the uses of self-defense, attack, and personal aggrandizement. From the myriad misinterpretations and misuses of our feelings arise many of our problems in relating—and thence our broader social ills, all the way from violent crime at home or in the streets to quiet crime in corporate offices.

To decode feelings and recover their original messages requires patience and practice. We need to keep asking ourselves how particular feelings can be interpreted in light of the four fundamental values. For instance, if we are angry at someone, is it because we are being treated unfairly or disrespectfully? If so, how can we communicate our concern *fairly and respectfully,* so that we do not repeat the mistakes of the person who has offended us? Or, if we feel uncomfortable with ourselves, is it because we are acting in an unfair or uncaring way? Compassionate self-exploration of this sort can show us the way out of a confusion of feelings that may paralyze our ability to make decisions and act powerfully.

Uncovering the Values Within

Jack was a successful businessman in his early fifties who'd been coming to me for self-change counseling for about a year. Unable to make a decision about severing a troublesome business partnership, Jack had reached the point of almost not speaking to the other man in this venture. But the financial consequences of dividing up their assets and clientele would be high. Deciding first to stick it out, then that it wasn't worth it, and then that he couldn't afford to leave, Jack spent weeks agonizing over the problem, finally telling me that he just couldn't get a clear answer from inside himself.

"All logic and material considerations aside," Jack said to me one day, "my feelings about this change every day. So I just can't rely on my feelings to sort this out, even if they do arise from my real spirit, as you say."

Knowing Jack, I suspected that his mixed-up feelings were due to his difficulty in connecting affirmative values to his feelings. So I tried to shift his vantage point radically on the whole situation by asking him to imagine a future time when his much-beloved son Kenneth would be his own age. "Now just try to picture Ken in your place in this situation, Jack. Let's say you're looking down from heaven and watching how Ken handles exactly the same situation. In the interest of Ken's well-being and self-respect, do you get a feeling about what you would want him to do regarding this partnership?"

Jack's reply was swift and succinct. "Oh, there's no question I'd want him to get out."

"Wait a minute!" I said incredulously. "Are you sure, Jack? In weeks of agonizing over this problem, you haven't had any clarity on this at all."

"Well, I'd hate to see my son put up with all this bullshit," Jack explained pungently.

The puzzle was solved. Jack couldn't make up his mind because he didn't know how to take care of his vulnerable spirit, and that's why he couldn't sort out the swirl of feelings that arose in reaction to the situation. But Jack was certain that his son was a good person who deserved respect, care, understanding, and fairness—and he knew what such a worthy person should do in the situation.

The point of this story is that the four fundamental values reside as latent potentials within us even when our feelings and thoughts no longer seem to reflect them. Rediscovering values can sometimes be a simple matter of *imagining* how we could make value-driven decisions and act to uphold them; the wisdom of our spirit can help us rediscover capacities we think we have lost or never possessed.

I often hear from men, for instance, that they don't know how to express tenderness toward their wives or children. They're used to being strong and capable, but not tender; they say—"It's just not me." So I ask such men to think about how they treat their sports car, computer, dog, or favorite fishing rod. Is there any thing or being close to them that evokes a warm, protective feeling?

I then ask them to imagine transferring the essence of that feeling to their wives or children, and to pay careful attention to any resistances that come up as they imagine it.

With few exceptions, resistance to expressing tender care for another person is connected to a dearth of demonstrative affection and comforting in one's childhood—and the closely related sense that one doesn't deserve tender caring oneself. As a result one learns to deny hurt, which results in anger, irritability, and resentment. Thus one's spirit is suppressed and distorted, and the messages it sends about needing and wanting to give care easily become garbled.

Using Values to Decode Feelings

It takes time and patience with oneself—and ethical communication with others—to decode the garbling of feelings and regain the values of the spirit in their native form. Whenever bad feelings arise, we can begin decoding them by asking ourselves such questions as:

- What is this bad feeling trying to draw my attention toward? Is there something I need to do to better respect or care for myself or others in this situation?
- Is this bad feeling an exaggeration of something important that I've been ignoring for a while? For instance, am I bitter about someone not listening to me because I haven't been speaking up for myself for a long time?
- Is there a part of this bad feeling that has some positive energy? For instance, do I feel violent because I want to shout or make big, dramatic movements, and I never give myself the opportunity for physical self-expression?
- Can I feel compassion for my pain even if I do not yet understand its source? Is there anything I can do right

now, in accord with the values of respect, understanding, caring, and fairness, to arrange some comforting for myself while I begin improving the situation in which these bad feelings have arisen?

Decoding of bad feelings takes a big step forward when you remember this simple principle from Chapter 2: *Bad feelings are messages from your inner spirit about something you need to change or pay attention to in your life. Bad feelings are not evidence of inner badness.* When bad feelings are interpreted as proof of personal unworthiness, the four fundamental values of your spirit have already been violated.

Good feelings generally don't need much decoding; they tend to be relatively clear and affirmative messages from the spirit. Brief rushes of giddiness or exaggerated pride can be distortions of our true spirit, however, and often presage a "crash" into negativity. Nor should good feelings be confused with temporary pleasures and sensations. Thrill-seeking is not a route to deep affirmation of self and others, although many people substitute the search for pleasure for the real work of building self-respect and caring relationships.

I've provided these basic guidelines on the decoding and management of feelings because they can be very useful when the time arrives to handle strong feelings during Ethical Persuasion. At certain stages you or another person may have to take time out to process strong feelings that have arisen in a conversation. Using these guidelines, you may be able not only to accelerate the understanding of your own feelings, but to help out the other person, too, if he or she seems open to considering your perspective on their situation. The more you can collaborate on the interpretation and positive management of the feelings going on between you, the greater the chances you have of creating masterful, synergistic resolutions in the final stage of EP.

Courage = A Little Willingness

Does all this talk about values imply that one must have a firm grasp of respect, understanding, caring, and fairness *before* Ethical Persuasion can be applied to serious conflicts? Absolutely not—on the contrary, EP is designed to be a learning and teaching tool for anyone who thinks the values are worth exploring as new guidelines for living and communicating. The values are not prerequisites for this course of learning; they are the very subject of study. You might call Ethical Persuasion "Applied Values 101."

What *is* required to undertake EP is courage. And what is courage? Nothing more than mustering a little willingness to consider the possibility of change—that life can be better, that people can have a greater understanding and connection, that we all have a great untapped potential for creativity and community. Courage is not the absence of fear, nor is it the ability to completely conquer our fears; it is the willingness to take a single step in the face of our fears. It is another fundamental quality of the human spirit. If we believe we do not have any courage, then we are only *preventing* ourselves from acting courageously because we choose to run from both our fear and our self-respect.

I can't think of a better illustration of this condition than the fearfulness of Fran, a woman in her midforties who came to me to learn how to assert herself in her second marriage. After two years of living with Steve, a successful real-estate broker who set the two of them up in a splendid and spacious home, Fran was beginning to feel like an in-house exile because two of Steve's adult children (and one of their significant others) had moved into the house at Steve's invitation—and with next to no consultation with Fran.

Privately, Fran felt compassion for Steve's children from his first marriage, both of them young and professionally adrift during an economic recession. But she wasn't certain that moving in with their father was the best thing for them in the long term. And she was increasingly resentful that Steve hadn't talked to her about it until after he'd invited his kids to come. He simply assumed that Fran would go along in a situation in which he felt he had little choice. The confidence, enthusiasm, and decisiveness that Fran had admired in her new husband from the beginning were now beginning to intimidate her.

I talked to Fran about how she could use Ethical Persuasion to let Steve know that she was uncomfortable in their home situation and that she needed to air her feelings about it. It would be best, I suggested, to begin by soliciting all of Steve's feelings—letting him know that her discomfort made it very important that she understand exactly how he had arrived at the decision to invite his kids to live with them. At this stage, it's important to be genuinely curious about another's perspective, and not critical or accusatory.

"Make sure you prove to Steve that you do understand his position thoroughly before you offer him the details of yours," I coached Fran. "It may seem backward, but it's really the best way to ensure a fair hearing for yourself later on."

Fran eyed me nervously and fidgeted with the purse she clutched in her lap. "That strategy sounds ideal, Tom, for a person who could muster up even a little courage." She sighed. "But just bringing up the subject terrifies me. I'm not a brave person."

"Fair enough," I replied. "You acknowledge that you're a person who feels a great deal of fear and terror. If I understand you correctly, you're saying that you feel so much fear around this situation that it's too much to confront even for the sake of your self-respect. The risk of hearing something frightening or painful outweighs your desire for respect and fair treatment—although those are the reasons you came here to consult me. Are you saying you're willing to go on trading in your self-respect in order to avoid pain and remain in Steve's protective custody?"

"Well . . ." Fran glanced at the door as if she were already looking for an escape route. "Maybe I can imagine *starting* the process, but I don't think I could keep it up through every step. What if the first thing Steve says is so completely reasonable that I'll sound really selfish? Or what if he gets mad?"

"Okay, wait a minute. I need to understand exactly what you're saying. Here's what it sounds like to me; correct me if I'm wrong. It sounds like you're saying that the Fran who's right here with me now could imagine saying, 'Help me understand you, Steve.' But you can also imagine that the Fran who hears the answer might not be able to handle it. Is that what you're saying?"

"Right," said Fran, smiling slightly, as if glad to have found an ally in her fearfulness.

But I was headed in another direction. "If that's the case, then what right does the Fran who's sitting here now— who *does* feel that she can ask the first question—what right does this Fran have to say what Fran at a later moment in time can handle? Why not give yourself the option of making different decisions in the future?"

"But I *know* what could happen," she whined.

"What's the worst thing that could happen?" I asked.

"Well, I could try this process, and then have to walk out crying and humiliated in the middle of it. Then everything would be worse than before."

"Help me understand why it would be worse."

"Because," Fran said softly, "I would have tried and failed."

I could suddenly feel a pitiful, childish sadness in the room. The ancient hurt that was driving Fran's passivity was showing its face, and at a later time she might benefit from exploring its origins. For the moment, I wanted to save time by helping Fran uncover and mobilize her courage.

The Secret Fear of Power

"No, Fran, I don't think you would have failed. You would have courageously tried and chosen *not to go on,* because the pain at that moment would be too great, and you have a right to choose how much pain you're willing to tolerate. Why is that a failure? If you take the first step, you've discovered and acted on your courage, regardless of what happens next. Demonstrating your courage is the very best way to show Steve that you want greater input."

"But Steve won't see my courage. He'll only see me give up and fail," Fran protested.

"Well, that may be true," I conceded. "He may even feel teased or confused by your soliciting his feelings and opinions, and then closing down the process when you can't handle what he says. But even if that happened, is that worse than his completely ignoring you, which is the situation at present? Do you want to continue running your life by getting out of everybody's way, or do you want to run your life by being true to yourself? Because I think that's the choice you're facing right now."

Fran stared at me momentarily as if she were deeply offended. Then she sat up in her chair a little straighter and spoke almost conspiratorially. "Okay, Tom, let me tell you the whole situation. Maybe I'm afraid to hear what Steve has to say because he already has all the power in the household. The thing is, if I open the door to a total understanding of why he let the kids move in, I'll just be encouraging him. Inviting him to explain himself will just increase his power; that's really the problem, to tell the truth. Maybe I don't have much power now, but I don't want to risk what little I have."

"I see what you mean," I said, nodding. "But doesn't a lot of Steve's power depend on your obedience and passivity? If you actively asserted yourself, he might suddenly appear not to have so much power. Perhaps he seems to have the power because you gave it to him! What I believe you two have is a high-tension *balance* of power—kind of a cold war, a standoff."

Fran looked away thoughtfully before replying. "Well, I have sectioned myself off in the household. I run my life and take care of certain things for all of us, but mostly I stay out of everybody's way. I'm just getting tired of it."

"I bet you are!" I sympathized. "But let me suggest the possibility that you're not afraid of starting a discussion because it could give Steve even more power. He's already got most of it. What little you have is the power of withdrawing into your cocoon and holding everybody at arm's length. I don't really think you're afraid of failing at Phase One of EP, that is, afraid of not being able to hear Steve out. I think you're actually afraid of Phase Two, having to come out of your cocoon and explain yourself. I suspect it terrifies you to imagine asserting a fair role for yourself, having to say what you want and how things make you feel. Tell me something, Fran. What if you told Steve everything you feel about this situation, and then as a result the two of you decided that the kids didn't belong in the household?"

Fran's face registered a brief look of panic before she replied. "Well, I think I'd feel terrible. I have a lot of sympathy for their problems, you know, and I wouldn't want to be forcing them out. . . ."

"Are you saying you wouldn't even want to be partially responsible for making such a powerful decision?"

Now Fran looked flustered and confused, and I decided to step into the breach with some understanding. "You see, Fran, I don't believe you're really afraid of Steve winning more power. I think you're afraid of having more power for yourself—because you're not used to it, and you're not used to being responsible for its consequences. But remember, the point is not to engage in a battle to take away all the power. Ethical Persuasion is a means for you to end the standoff, start finding ways to share power with Steve, be closer and have a better working partnership. You might be surprised to learn how much Steve would like to have your input, or how puzzled he is by your withdrawal. Once you and Steve have a better understanding, you could even bring his kids into the discussion and then you might all come up with a creative resolution for this problem. You don't have to be responsible for everything—just your fair share.

"I think this issue of courage will be a lot easier for you, Fran, as you begin to understand why your upset feelings have brought you to this point. You consulted me because you want to feel respected, understood, cared about, and treated fairly at home—just the way you excel at treating everyone else. Are you willing to take the first little step toward that possibility, no matter how scary it is? Are you ready to start feeling brave and more in control of your life? Is it worth the risk?''

Part II

How Does Ethical Persuasion Work?

N ow you are ready to begin learning the hands-on techniques of Ethical Persuasion. This part of the book presents three simple phases of EP: "Learning the Other Person's Viewpoint," "Explaining Your Viewpoint," and "Creating Resolutions." You'll find sample phrases and a number of examples for each phase. It may be useful for you first to apply EP in your imagination, adapting some sample phrases to a crucial communication that you create in your own mind or write out on paper. Or you may choose to role-play an Ethical Persuasion scenario with an interested friend or co-worker. Such rehearsals can be invaluable before you begin to apply EP to a real-life encounter.

"Exploring the Other Person's Viewpoint" is by far the most important phase of EP and the aspect of communication that most people fail to pursue adequately. Become skillful at convincing others that you thoroughly understand their point of view and appreciate their feelings, and you will possess the key to Ethical Persuasion. Often, adequately completing Phases 1 and 2 will make Phase 3 unnecessary—because most of the problems of human beings in relationship arise from a lack of mutual understanding. With understanding, people can muster the determination, creativity, and cooperation necessary to solve their most serious problems.

4

Phase 1: Exploring the Other Person's Viewpoint

Most people struggling through difficult communications think they are better listeners than they really are. At best they allow another person to state their case, and then they make their own private interpretation of what the other person has said. At worst they are preparing their own argument *while* the other person is still talking. Unfortunately, most of us are more likely to react to our own interpretations of another's point of view than to do whatever is necessary to make certain that we thoroughly understand.

The first phase of Ethical Persuasion counteracts this common tendency with seven deliberate steps toward gaining a full understanding of another person's thoughts *and* feelings. A full understanding is guaranteed by taking the time to state the other person's position in your own words, then asking that person to correct or affirm the way you've restated their thoughts and feelings. You repeat this process of explicit confirmation until the other person has no doubt that you grasp their position completely. The more heated the exchange is emotionally, the more thorough you should be in restating and confirming what the other person has to say.

Why Should You Listen First?

Even when you are the one who is initiating a discussion about something of concern to you, it will be advantageous to explore the other person's viewpoint fully before you present yours in detail. While it's necessary to make clear to another person exactly what you want to talk about— and how concerned you are about the subject—there are distinct advantages to holding your tongue after that point and listening to the other person.

Of course, someone may have questions for you as they state their viewpoint, and you should answer them as straightforwardly as possible—resisting, however, the temptation to plunge into all of your concerns and feelings at the first opportunity. While give and take naturally occurs during all phases of Ethical Persuasion, the *emphasis* of Phase 1 is on exploring fully what the other person has to say. Whatever you say during this phase should further that purpose.

What are the advantages of listening first? Here are four that I know of, although you may discover more:

• *Learning from the other person's presentation of his or her thoughts and feelings.* If you're very upset about something, it may not have occurred to you that you don't have all the facts, didn't get the right story, or are simply mistaken about what the other person feels, believes, or has done. By asking for the other person's explanation *before* you air all your reactions to the situation you've presumed to be true, you may save yourself some embarrassment. And you may save everyone involved a lot of arguing over errors, distortions, and misinterpretations that are much more difficult to correct after someone has become defensive.

Even if you have the facts straight and your concerns are perfectly legitimate, the opportunity to witness what other people say and how they say it can be an invaluable tool for shaping your own statements. You also have the simple advantage of knowing both sides of the discussion *before* it's your turn to speak.

• *Earning the leverage of fairness.* By demonstrating the patience and openness to hear out the other person completely, you are earning the right to request and expect a full hearing of your viewpoint later. (This kind of fairness is a far cry from just taking turns shouting at each other, and has significant advantages over the back-and-forth approach of "active listening.") The more thorough you are in listening, and in checking out your understanding of the other person, the more likely that person will be to treat you similarly when your turn comes.

• *Defusing any negative effects of another person's pent-up feelings.* If you are initiating EP because you are aware of strong negative feelings coming from another person, then your willingness to listen first will show that you are respectfully deferring to the urgency of those feelings. By receiving another person's agitated concern with appreciation and understanding—instead of any defensiveness or knee-jerk retaliation—you will show that the relationship as a whole is more important to you than the particular issue at hand. Following the release of his or her pent-up feelings, the other person will calm down and become more reasonable and open to hearing you. It takes two to make a fight. By opting out of the first round, you can demonstrate your capacity to lead an exchange to higher ground.

• *Cultivating your patience, openness, and objectivity under stress.* Any time you can demonstrate your willingness to listen to someone with a minimum of self-defensiveness or criticism, you are cultivating virtues within yourself that have a high payoff in self-respect. Any significant personal change requires exactly this kind of courage: the willingness to feel uncomfortable while acting "as if" one is more mature and capable than one's familiar self. In this sense, Ethical Persuasion fertilizes the seeds of strong character within its practitioners.

The Seven Steps

For easy reference, all seven steps of Phase 1 of Ethical Persuasion are listed following this paragraph. A discussion of each step follows, complete with key phrases that you may be able to use or modify in actual conversations. In all situations, remember that the goal of Phase 1 is *to convince the other person that you thoroughly understand their thoughts and feelings.*

The Seven Steps of
Exploring the Other Person's Viewpoint

1. Establish that your immediate goal is mutual understanding, not problem solving.

2. Elicit the other person's thoughts, feelings, and desires about the subject at hand.
3. Ask for the other person's help in understanding him or her. Try not to defend or disagree.
4. Repeat the other person's position in your own words to show you understand.
5. Ask the other person to correct your understanding and keep restating his or her position.
6. Refer back to your position only to keep things going.
7. Repeat steps 1 through 6 until the other person unreservedly agrees that you understand his or her position.

───────

1. Establish that your immediate goal is mutual understanding, not problem solving. This preparatory step is enormously important in "reducing the steam" that may have arisen in a serious conflict, and in helping people to focus on the *quality of their relationship at the moment* rather than the apparent problem at hand. (In many cases, the quality of the relationship probably is the source of the problem, as well as the key to its resolution.)

When you realize that a communication is in trouble and Ethical Persuasion is called for, a good opening may be:

"Look, it feels to me like things are getting out of hand. Can we back up a little and first make sure we really understand each other?"

Or:

"I don't feel like we're getting anywhere with this problem. Can we put a hold on finding a practical solution for the moment,

and simply compare our points of view in more detail? I'd be happy to let you expand on your position first."

Or:

"For now, can we agree to begin by understanding each other thoroughly, and then worry about where to go from there?"

Or:

"I think I need to step back and get clear on exactly what you're trying to say to me. Perhaps my feelings have gotten in the way of my really hearing you."

Affirming that understanding is your first priority not only helps you focus on the relationship at hand, but also reduces some of the anxiety and competitiveness that may have arisen in a conflicted situation. Under stress, many people will limit or arrange what they have to say according to their moment-to-moment assessment of whether they are "winning" the discussion. They will pick and choose among their feelings and thoughts, or even distort the facts at their disposal, in whatever way that strikes them as strategically superior.

The best way to defuse this kind of strategizing is to acknowledge the likelihood that everyone involved in a difficult discussion feels insecure and threatened. It's both disarming and very powerful to admit your own vulnerability as your primary motive for seeking mutual understanding. You might put it this way:

"I just don't like the direction that this discussion is going. I'm getting pretty upset, and it looks to me like you may be upset, too. Can we take a few minutes to explain our feelings to each other? I'd really appreciate hearing how you feel about this right now."

Or:

"I get the feeling that you're more upset with this discussion than you're letting on. I'd hate to make a decision that's really

not good for both/all of us, so can we pursue a little more un-derstanding of each other and put the decision aside for a little while?"

Or:

"Just because I'm the boss/father/mother doesn't mean I want to make everybody unhappy with a bad decision. Let's make sure we first understand each other and then we'll see if we can't work this out together."

2. Elicit the other person's thoughts, feelings, and desires about the subject at hand. If you're initiating a conversation about something, this step will be automatic and may occur simultaneously with Step 1. Remember that you want to establish clearly the subject of the discussion, revealing the *degree* of your concern about it, without going into all of your thoughts and feelings first. You can start with something as simple as:

"I have a problem and would appreciate your help."

Or:

"I need to be certain that I understand what you want to happen as a result of our meeting/project/relationship."

Or:

"I heard about the new promotions and I have to admit that I'm pretty upset about being passed over. Could you explain to me how these decisions were made, so that I have a grasp of the whole situation?"

Or:

"I'm upset with the way you behaved at the party. It made me jealous. But before I go into all that, I need to make sure I understand what you were feeling. Can you tell me about the party from your point of view?"

Or:

"Your grades have been sliding this semester, and we've heard *from the school that you've missed some classes. This is very upsetting to us, and we need to know what the problem is. We're afraid we may have gotten out of touch, and we can't help you if we don't understand what's going on. Can you fill us in on how things are going?"*

If you're attempting to redirect a conversation that has started to go awry because strong feelings are heating up on one or both sides, it's important to acknowledge those feelings. If the other person seems to be getting upset first, as soon as you notice it you can say something like:

"Am I doing or saying something/not doing or saying something that creates a problem for you?"

Or:

"You seem to be upset/unhappy/irritated with me. Am I wrong?"

If you notice that *you're* getting upset while the other person remains calm, it may be a little harder to initiate EP. You'll have to hold back the force of your feelings while you thoroughly sound out the other person. This does *not* mean, however, that you should pretend you're not upset. You may gain tremendous leverage, in fact, if you can honestly acknowledge your feelings *and* make it clear that the other person's input takes priority over the full expression of your own discomfort. You might put it this way:

"Look, I have to tell you that I'm beginning to feel uncomfortable/a little upset about this. So I need to be especially careful to make sure that I really understand what you're saying."

Or:

"Wait a minute. Something about the direction we're going just doesn't feel right to me. Perhaps I misunderstand. Would you mind going over what you've said so far?"

3. Ask for the other person's help in understanding him or her. Try not to defend or disagree. This step goes against the grain of most people's habitual way of relating under pressure. We may have no problem in respectfully soliciting another's thoughts and feelings at the outset of an encounter. But when things start to get intense, we will tend to break into the middle of what another person is saying to give our immediate reaction. The other person reacts to our reaction, and soon the whole conversation has derailed. In the rush to *vent* feelings, we actually fail to *respect* feelings—our own and those of other people. The idea of EP is to operate on a rational basis that makes full use of feelings as important data, instead of merely suppressing them or giving in to them entirely.

Most of us are far more sensitive and vulnerable than we like to admit to ourselves, especially around certain issues related to earlier emotional wounds. As a result, we can unexpectedly overreact in the form of unnecessary self-defense or unwarranted counterattack. As Chapter 2 explained, feelings begin as private messages from our own deep inner spirit about whether something is right for us. Skillful use of the vital information that feelings provide pays off by enhancing self-understanding. For a number of reasons, feelings are messages that usually have to be decoded to be fruitfully understood—and that takes some time and self-restraint.

Thus, this third step may require holding your immediate reactions in check while you pursue a thorough understanding of what the other person means. Since you are not the expert on the other person's position, you must ask for the expert's help. You might do it this way:

"I think I hear what you're saying, but I want to double-check. Do you mean that . . ."

Or:

"I'm well aware that I might be quite wrong about what's going on, so I need you to explain. . . ."

Or:

"Maybe I'm jumping to conclusions, but to me what you're saying means that . . . Exactly how do you mean it? / How does it feel to you? / Am I getting it right?"

Or:

"Apparently you see me as the person responsible for hurting you / causing the problem. Please explain further, because this upsets me and I need to understand."

4. Repeat the other person's position in your own words to show you understand. While training myself in Ethical Persuasion, I learned the importance of this step in a pivotal conversation I had with my wife, Judy, some years ago. We had been working on our tendency to withdraw from each other when one of us became upset. I was usually the one to provoke the pattern; when I felt bad about something, I would become sullen and quiet. Judy would react by avoiding me, and then the cycle would feed on itself, intensifying for days at a time. Soon our communication would be limited to snapping at each other with great irritation, causing a drain of energy for both of us.

So one day I asked her, "Why do you avoid me and get angry with me when I'm upset about something? I don't understand why you need me to be happy all the time."

"That's not it," Judy replied. "I just can't deal with you when you're angry."

Usually I would have retorted with something like, "Well, what makes me angry is . . ." This time I decided to pursue a further understanding of her feelings, initiating

Ethical Persuasion: "What do you mean, you can't deal with me?"

"When you get sullen and withdrawn," Judy explained, "I always feel like you're ready to explode. It makes me very tense and uncomfortable."

"You're afraid I'd explode if you were to ask me what's going on?" I asked, repeating her position in my own words.

"Yes," she said. "When I've tried to ask you what's wrong, you sound so irritated and angry that I'd rather just leave you alone. So I do."

At this point, Judy's tone of voice was giving me as much information as her words. It influenced me to restate her position in another way: "So what you're saying is that when I get upset you become afraid of me—and maybe also angry with me because I'm scaring you."

"It's more than that," she answered.

"How so?"

"When you're withdrawn and irritated, you're actually pushing me away," Judy pointed out. "At least that's how it feels to me."

"So when I'm upset and withdrawn, you think I'm rejecting you," I offered. "Just my *being upset* hurts you."

"Exactly," Judy said.

This was the first time I had really understood why Judy reacted the way she did to my being upset—why she couldn't offer solace for my feelings, or even truly "leave me alone" to sort them out without an air of hostility in the household. Knowing her side, especially her vulnerable feelings, helped me. It didn't solve the whole problem; I still had to figure out the reasons I became upset, and how to talk about them in a way that would elicit Judy's support. But this conversation was a key step in the process of our finding a way to work on this problem cooperatively.

In your own conversations, repeating the other person's view to make certain you understand extends a courtesy that others may not be used to receiving. So you will probably want to inform them of what you are doing by saying something like:

"Okay, I want to make sure that I've got this straight. You're saying that . . . Have I got that right? / Is that correct?"

Or:

"It's important to me that I really understand. Let me see if I can put what you're saying into my own words."

Or:

"So what you're saying is . . ."

In heated discussions, repeating someone's position in your own words can be a real challenge to your objectivity. If you feel yourself becoming patronizing or sarcastic, it may be helpful to remember that these attitudes are almost always forms of self-defense. To indulge them distorts the other person's position with your own feelings, which you will have a better chance to express clearly and directly later. But neither is it fruitful to invest your restatement of another's feelings with a false warmth or forced kindness. Your tone of voice doesn't have to prove that you're a caring person; your pursuit of Ethical Persuasion is proof enough of that. Just try for the clearest possible restatement of another person's thoughts and feelings.

5. Ask the other person to correct your understanding and keep restating his or her position. If your statement of the other person's ideas or feelings doesn't sound right to them, they may betray this in their facial expression or say

"No, that's not what I mean" or "That's not quite right." If you hear such a comment, don't rush to make additional guesses about their position, or make the mistake of trying to *tell them* what they mean. It actually streamlines the process—and convinces others of your sincerity and respect—if you simply acknowledge their reaction and ask for further clarification. Ways to do this might include:

"Well, I guess I'm not quite with you yet. Could you explain further about . . ."

Or:

"Okay, I need to back up a little. What exactly did you mean when you said . . ."

Or:

"Sorry—I guess I'm jumping to conclusions. Tell me a little bit more about . . . , so I can get this straight."

After you've solicited further explanations, you can make another try at restating the other person's position in your own words. Three things are accomplished in this repetitive process: refining your own understanding, demonstrating your determination to treat the other person fairly, and giving the other person an opportunity to clarify their thoughts and feelings. The more that others are convinced of your sincerity and follow-through, the more likely they are to treat you just as well in Phase 2, when you explain your viewpoint. The awareness that a job well done in Phase 1 will give you moral leverage helps make up for any discomfort of emotional self-restraint that may be required of you. At this step, you may preface your continuing attempts to restate another's position like this:

"Now that I'm a little clearer on this, let me take another stab at putting it in my own words."

Or:

"Thanks for steering me right on this. Let me know whether I've got it straight now. The way I would describe your position is . . ."

6. Refer back to your position only to keep things going.
This step is really a rule of thumb that may be relevant at any time during Phase 1. A situation may arise in which another person is unlikely to explain their full position without hearing part of yours, or challenges what they assume to be your viewpoint while explaining theirs: "I'll tell you how I feel—I feel like you don't really care what happens one way or another! Am I wrong about that?" Rather than refusing such a challenge, you can make an abbreviated disclosure of what you think and feel: "If I didn't care, would I be trying to give you a fair hearing right now?" Note that this reply also reaffirms the values that drive Ethical Persuasion in the first place.

Throughout Phase 1, the goal is to maintain a respectful conversation that is weighted toward revelation of the other person's viewpoint. You want to strike a balance between withholding your position as if it were a secret, and getting into a rapid exchange of opinions that outraces your capacity to understand the other person's major concerns. Of course, if you are initiating the exchange because of your own concerns, a brief statement of your position will be necessary just to "prime the pump" and get things going. But beware of the temptation to jump the gun by beginning to air all your concerns before the next and final step of Phase 1 is completed. To make it clear that you're setting limits on your own disclosure at this point, you may say:

"Since you've asked, I'll be happy to tell you briefly what I

have been thinking/feeling about this. But then I'd like to get back to what you were saying."

Or:

"I want to make absolutely certain that I understand you before we get into my side of things. But to answer your question . . ."

Or:

"I'm bringing this up because I'm concerned about . . . But first I'd like to hear your side of things."

7. Repeat steps 1 through 6 until the other person unreservedly agrees that you understand his or her position. This step directs you to cycle back through all the previous steps until there is *no doubt* in your own mind *and* the other person's mind that you understand their position completely. How do you make sure? Again, you ask the expert, the person who knows that position thoroughly because it is their own. Resist the temptation to say "Okay, I've got it!" and instead use such expressions as:

"Let me see if I can summarize what I believe you've been trying to get me to hear. Please correct any misperceptions on my part."

Or:

"I feel like I may be getting the gist of what you're saying. Let me lay it out for you one more time in my own words, and feel free to let me know if anything's even a little off."

Or:

"I really want to thank you for being so patient with me while I was trying to learn how you see things. Here's how I would sum up your position."

At this culminative stage, the response you're looking for will be something like "Yes, you've got it" or "Exactly!" or even "Okay, I'm more than convinced that you understand me! Can we please move on?" The irritation of being too well understood is so rare and momentary that you needn't fear provoking it. Few people have lasting resentment about being listened to in a respectful way.

Typical Difficulties of Phase 1

Practicing and teaching Ethical Persuasion have shown me that people who initiate the process may experience four different kinds of difficulty during the phase of learning another's position. These difficulties occur as *resistances* within oneself. The first is the *difficulty of restraining strong feelings* while giving another person a full hearing. When disagreement, hurt, or anger are provoked by what another person is saying, it seems only natural to respond immediately with a correction, an expression of dismay, or some attempt at self-defense.

That's when it's important to remember that EP is *not* a natural or instinctive process—it is a deliberate and artificial approach to negotiation based on conscious commitment to the values of respect, understanding, caring, and fairness. This means that while some steps of the process may feel unnatural and awkward, they are undertaken with a sincere desire to increase mutual honesty and understanding. This is not the same as pretending that you feel or believe something you do not.

The situation is similar to that of learning a foreign language. When you repeat words and phrases you do not fully understand for the sake of learning, you are not being dishonest or phony. But you will feel silly and awkward for a while until the new language becomes second nature to you. In much the same way, practicing the deliberate steps of EP will eventually make them feel natural, and your use of them will be continually reinforced by your success in important communications and the general enhancement of all your relationships.

If the going gets tough because of your own strong feelings, it may be helpful to acknowledge that you are deliberately applying this special, artificial process:

"Look, what you're saying has got me pretty upset, and normally I'd just blow my stack at this point. But I'm trying to get better at hearing others out completely instead of just shooting my mouth off. So please continue. After we've made absolutely certain that I understand your point of view completely, you can bet I'll ask you to do the same for me, and allow me to have my say!"

Contrast this kind of candid self-disclosure to the covertness of popular communication strategies such as "keep smiling" and "use the other person's first name frequently." (Another, even more insidious technique is to preface all responses to another person with "You're right," whether you agree with them or not.) When feelings are intense, these social ploys can be particularly irritating and counterproductive. It's better to be able to admit that you're following a method of communication that uses no subliminal manipulations.

Another common resistance to the learning phase of EP is the *fear that explicit understanding implies giving in.* It's my observation that many people equate saying "I understand you" with "I surrender." I saw this clearly when counseling Jay and Amelia, a husband and wife who told me about a conflict they had while visiting his parents for a week at a resort. His mother was very critical and controlling of the grandchildren and began harping about the kids' language, clothes, and anything else she could think of as soon as the family arrived. Amelia wasted no time in telling her mother-in-law to back off. "We've just arrived for our vacation and I don't want things to start off this way. Can you just let the kids be kids for a change?"

In response Jay's mother exploded as if she were the victim: "I guess I never do anything right in your eyes, Amelia. You just got here and you're already criticizing me!" At this point both women turned to Jay, whose only response was to walk away saying, "Hey, leave me out of this." Amelia was furious when she confronted Jay later in private: "Don't you see what your mother's doing, attacking the kids and then pretending to be innocent?"

Jay then told his wife "I just don't see why it upsets you so much," which didn't help matters. But when he doggedly repeated this to Amelia in my office, I suspected that it wasn't quite true.

"Wait a minute, Jay," I said. "Let me make sure I'm clear about this. Are you saying that you really don't understand why Amelia gets upset when your mother talks that way to the kids? Is that what you're saying?"

"Yeah," he replied. "I don't see why it bothers her so much. We all know how my mother is—why do we have to keep getting upset about it?"

"Let me put it more dramatically," I suggested. "If I offered you a million bucks to explain, right now, why Amelia is upset about this, could you do it? Or would you have to turn down the money because you don't have the slightest idea about her feelings?"

"Okay, okay," said Jay. "I know Amelia hates to see the kids take all this stuff from my mom. It hurts her to watch it and it hurts her that we can't all get along. And it probably makes her mad that I walk away and don't stand up for her. Maybe it seems that I don't even care about the kids *or* her." By now Amelia was staring at Jay in amazement, dumbfounded by the revelation of his empathy.

"So why are you saying that you don't understand, Jay?" I asked. "It sounds like you understand Amelia pretty well."

"That's just great," he replied in exasperation. "So that means I'm supposed to stand up to my mother next time and start an even bigger fight! Then the kids will lose their grandparents completely. That's great, just great!"

"Whoa!" I countered. "It doesn't mean any such thing. You don't have to fight anybody, Jay. All we're trying to determine is whether you *understand* Amelia—not whether you agree with what she wants you to do, assuming that is what she wants."

As further discussion revealed, Amelia didn't want Jay simply to join the fighting; mostly she wanted him to acknowledge her feelings, to show her his caring and concern, and to know that they could discuss such family problems openly together. Jay's fear that admitting his understanding implied some kind of capitulation on his part is common, especially for the type of man used to seeing all negotiations as power struggles.

Related to this "fear of understanding" is the simple fear of being wrong—*the perceived risk of realizing that you're mistaken about something and may have to admit it.* There can be a tendency to resist giving another person a full hearing because you're afraid of becoming convinced that they're closer to the right track than you are even before you begin to explain yourself. This fear may have some basis in fact—you may sense that your position is really not very strong, despite your emotional attachment to it—or your fear may stem from a sense of weakness, a habitual insecurity about yourself and your point of view.

Finally, Phase 1 of Ethical Persuasion can bring up the fear of *hearing something you don't want to face*. It may be something as plain as another's negative opinions of you, or it may be more indirect: perhaps a friend's revelation of their difficulties in an intimate relationship will remind you of your own. In either case, the less capacity you have developed for regarding your own pain with compassion, the more you will want to avoid bad news and painful information or insights.

Whatever their roots, the cure for difficulties in Phase 1 of EP is the same: courage. You can renew and refresh your own bravery by remembering that you have undertaken Ethical Persuasion as a route to greater understanding, the creative resolution of differences, and improved relationships—not to win battles or temporarily shore up a faltering sense of self-esteem. With greater understanding may come some uncomfortable discoveries: that you've been holding on to useless or outmoded beliefs; that you need to learn to speak up for yourself even though "keeping the peace" is your preferred style; that you don't have to be afraid of being challenged; or any of a thousand other realizations.

But along with the difficulties, Phase 1 brings a tremendous tactical advantage to anyone who initiates it. Whether your tone of voice is loving, tentative, grudging, or adversarial, the ethical advantage of hearing out another person fully, before you state your case, remains the same. The best way of earning someone's rapt attention is to give them the rare experience of being fully heard and understood.

5

Phase 2: Explaining Your Viewpoint

A street-smart saying in the mental health field reminds therapists to "Meet people where they are." This advice is equally sound for anyone seeking to get the most out of crucial communications. Whether you're talking to a child or teenager, housewife or engineer, it's best to know as much as you can about the other person's worldview and feelings. Then you can phrase your own viewpoint in a way that will be more readily appreciated than if you talk down to another or speak with the assumption that your way of seeing things is naturally the right one.

If you've completed Phase 1 of Ethical Persuasion, you can be sure that you've met another person where he or she is because you've gone to some trouble to confirm your understanding of the perspective, feelings, and language of that person. You haven't merely given someone a fair hearing; you've repeated their position in your own words, and asked for confirmation that you've gotten things right. If you've done this well, you've learned something important that you didn't know before, something likely to throw a new light on your own viewpoint before you've even stated it. This is the point at which EP begins to improve and deepen the relationship at hand—well before solutions are developed for any specific problems.

The Five Steps of Phase 2

Several principles are important to keep in mind as you learn the five steps of Phase 2 of Ethical Persuasion. First, it's crucial to remember that you are indeed the center of your private world, but not the *whole* world. This is the best possible stance for beginning to state your viewpoint, according respect both to your experience as an individual and to the other person's world of experience as well.

Second, the merging of people's private worlds that will occur during the EP process can be a profoundly moving (or shaking) experience that takes some time to integrate. It's best to allow as much time as possible for reflection at all stages of Ethical Persuasion, and to acknowledge that the ongoing process is bringing up information and insights that will have to be digested by both parties at a later time. If you can't actually take a break between hearing the other person's viewpoint and stating your own, then it's always helpful to acknowledge that what you've just heard is already influencing your viewpoint. Thus, whatever thoughts and feelings you're about to relate are already a little dated; they are what you brought to the table before Phase 1 was undertaken.

Finally, it's advantageous to make use of what you've

heard in Phase 1 to state your viewpoint in a way that makes it most likely to be heard and understood. This is what I call effective "packaging" of your position. Use some starting point from the other person's perspective ("I see why you're upset with me" or "Now that I know what you care about, let me say first that . . .") to introduce your thoughts and feelings. Whenever possible, compare and contrast elements of your experience with relevant elements of the other person's in order to keep in touch with their world even as you relate your own.

Following these ground rules will add depth and power to your presentation as it proceeds through the steps of Phase 2 of Ethical Persuasion, as follows.

The Five Steps of Explaining Your Viewpoint

1. Ask for a fair hearing in return.
2. Begin with an explanation of how the other person's thoughts and feelings affect you. Avoid blaming and self-defense as much as possible.
3. Carefully explain your thoughts, desires, and feelings as *your* truth, not *the* truth.
4. Ask for restatements of your position—and corrections of any factual inaccuracies—as necessary.
5. Review your respective positions.

---

1. Ask for a fair hearing in return. When you initiated Phase 1 of EP, you established that your immediate goal was mutual understanding, not problem solving. Then you made sure you understood the other person's view in full. Now you are positioned to ask for the same treatment in return. You're not interested in claiming a victory for yourself alone, affixing blame to either side, or establishing "right" or "wrong." You can claim your right to a fair hearing by saying something like:

"Now that you honestly feel that I understand how you think and feel, would you be willing to try to understand/let me explain my position on this?"

Or:

"Now that I understand what you think and feel, and why, would you be willing to do the same for me?"

Or:

"Fair is fair. Now will you please hear me out?"

Or:

"What you've just said is going to make me rethink my view of things. But are you willing to let me run through what I was thinking and feeling when I came in here today? I want you to understand where I've been coming from, even if I start to change my mind."

If you encounter initial resistance to the presentation of your viewpoint, you may want to press on the issue of fairness, taking advantage of the leverage you've gained from letting the other person state his or her position first. Imagine, for instance, that reviewing the full range of their feelings has made someone realize how angry they are with you, and despite your efforts to certify that you understand their anger, they're not inclined to let you state your case. You could then answer with something like:

"I understand that you're very upset with me. But is it fair for you not to give me as sincere and complete a hearing as I just gave you?"

Or:

"Look, I realize that going into this problem is not easy for either one of us. But I don't know of a better way to sort things out than to make sure we really understand each other. I've heard you out, and you've agreed that I have a pretty good idea of what you're thinking and feeling. In the interest of being fair and working this out, are you willing to let me speak my piece?"

For approaches to even tougher situations—when someone responds that they're not interested in fairness, for example—see Chapter 10, "Difficult People and Extra-Difficult Situations."

If you find it difficult to ask for a fair hearing because you're afraid of being tongue-tied and inarticulate when it's your turn to speak, you may find it helpful to do some preparatory work before an EP encounter. For instance, writing out your point of view, and specifying what you'd like to see happen as a result of an upcoming discussion, may help you feel better prepared when the time comes for you to speak. You might also rehearse the most difficult things you have to say out loud a number of times until you like the way it sounds. Say what you really think and feel, but try to package your message carefully, experimenting with the kind of language that you think will most easily be understood by the person with whom you will eventually have the real discussion.

Beware, however, of creating and depending upon an exact script in lieu of your own authentic speech in a face-to-face situation. Scripts memorized the night before can suddenly become outdated when you've just heard another person's point of view in Phase 1—particularly if the other person surprises you in any way. Then you could end up more at a loss than if you had never scripted yourself! Writing or rehearsing your point of view should primarily serve your own self-understanding and sense of readiness.

When the time comes to speak, you just have to go with the best you've got at the time.

The best way to handle your own awkwardness or in-articulateness *during* an encounter is to admit it openly and respectfully ask for the patience and forbearance of others. By preparing them for any difficulty you may have in expressing yourself, you stand a good chance of enlisting your discussion partners in your Phase 2 effort. This is a way to create strength from your own vulnerability. You could say:

"Before we go any further, I have to confess that sometimes I get my words mixed up when I'm trying to explain myself, especially if my feelings are running strong. I hope you can bear with me."

Or:

"You've done so well expressing yourself that I'm a little embarrassed to tell you my side of things. I'm not nearly so articulate. If you can be patient with the way my tongue gets tied up sometimes, I'll do my best to explain myself."

Or:

"Do you mind if we take a little break before I start to talk? You've expressed yourself very well and given me a lot to think about, and I'm not very fast on my feet. We'll probably save time and avoid confusion if I can organize my thoughts and get back to you in an hour/next week/the next time we meet."

Or:

"Now that you've made yourself clear, I'm upset/troubled/ pretty confused, and I don't think I'm ready to respond coherently. If it's okay with you, I'd like to take some time to think this over, and write you a letter about all this. That would be a tremendous help to me in making myself clear. Then we can meet and talk again. Is that all right?"

2. Begin with an explanation of how the other person's thoughts and feelings affect you. Avoid blaming and self-defense as much as possible. This step initiates the crucial connection between another person's private world of experience and your own. The objective here is not to analyze or pass judgment on another's viewpoint, which you worked hard to grasp in Phase 1, but to let them know how it influences your own thoughts and feelings. If your reaction is strong, you will likely experience some temptation to blame the other person for any bad feelings you have, or jump into a self-defensive stance because you perceive their viewpoint as an attack on you. Resisting this temptation as much as possible means trying to come up with words that will do justice to your strong feelings without misusing their energy to mount an offensive of your own. You might say something like:

"I hate the fact that you're so upset, because it makes me upset, too. I hope we can try to understand and not criticize each other. While I state my case, I'd appreciate it if you alert me to anything that sounds like I'm blaming you for the problem, because I know that won't be productive."

Or:

"I have to admit that I'm surprised to learn you've been feeling so hurt/angry/resentful about this situation. I feel badly about it, and I guess I have some catching up to do. I'd like to get a better understanding than we've had so far. I'm pretty sure that blaming each other won't do any good."

Or:

"Well, I'm not at all surprised by how you feel about this problem. I'm pretty disturbed about it myself, but knowing exactly how you feel makes everything a little less confusing. Now that I understand you better, let me see if I can tell you my side

of things without getting too defensive. I've been down that road before, and it doesn't lead anywhere."

Or:

"If I'd understood you this well before, maybe we wouldn't have this problem right now. I appreciate your honesty. What you've said is going to have a big effect on my whole point of view, so keep in mind that what I'm about to say is already becoming outdated. But up until I heard you out today, this is how I've been looking at things."

This last alternate addresses the possibility that the understanding you've reached of another's viewpoint in Phase 1 is sufficiently surprising to have a strong influence on your viewpoint even before you've had a chance to state it. In such cases, it can be important to review for the other person what you were thinking and feeling about the problem at hand until you heard them out. Of course, you will feel some awkwardness in admitting that your opinion and feelings are changing even as you speak, but you shouldn't assume this to be a sign of weakness on your part. On the contrary, it is a sign of admirable openness, flexibility, and sensitivity to the needs of others. Openness is *not* capitulation. Sharing your past and current feelings with the other person as honestly and nondefensively as possible is always a sign of inner strength.

3. Carefully explain your thoughts, desires, and feelings as your *truth*, not *the* truth. This step allows for a full and passionate presentation of how you see and feel about the situation under discussion. However, you need to recognize that your vision of the truth may not be applicable outside your personal world of experience. Keep in mind that the passionate certainty anyone feels and expresses about their point of view does not prove its correctness in terms of objective truth. Fair, creative resolutions come about only through the sharing and ethical synthesis of ideas—not the victory of one viewpoint over another.

It's easy to see that the failure to acknowledge that people see the world differently fuels the animosity behind some of our society's most painful controversies, including issues like abortion and the debate over censorship versus free expression. If we ever hope to resolve these bitter debates without ignoring or victimizing some portion of the populace, we will have to learn how to speak our piece without assuming that we have laid claim to The Truth, now and forevermore. For many, this will mean learning to place their faith in the process of honest, respectful communication rather than religious or social doctrines.

Step 3 of stating your viewpoint can be initiated by saying:

"Please bear with me. I'm not saying that I'm right or you're wrong. I'm simply trying to get you to understand how strongly I feel about this and why."

Or:

"I hope we can temporarily put aside worrying about whether we agree on what's right. Let's just try to really understand each other's feelings and point of view on this."

Or:

"Now I'd like to try to explain what's going on with me. Would you be willing to let me think out loud about my position on this?"

If you're ever uncertain about where to start with the presentation and exploration of your viewpoint, a good rule of thumb is to start with your fears. This means revealing your vulnerability, an aspect of the human spirit that everyone shares and that, properly seen, represents the potential for shared strength rather than our individual weakness. Vulnerability is not a fault or soft spot; it's the combination of our needs and sensitivities, and we are weakened only by attempting to *hide* it.

For instance, let us say that a man with a tendency to stutter when he is under pressure has to deliver a speech to a civic club. Will he be better off by admitting his impediment at the beginning of his talk and asking for the patience of the audience if his problem crops up, or by hoping that he can get through without having to discuss this aspect of his vulnerability? If he does the latter, he runs the risk of embarrassing himself (and the audience) far more than if he used his vulnerability to establish a respectful bond with his listeners at the outset.

The same principle applies to explaining your viewpoint. By offering up your honest uncertainties to another, you can establish contact points for mutual understanding. You can do this by saying:

"Look, I have to admit that I came into this worrying about . . . Having heard you out has helped me feel a little better, but I still need to share my concerns about . . ."

Or:

"Now that I know what you've been thinking and feeling, I'm doubly aware that I'm very sensitive to the issue of . . . Here's how I feel about it."

Or:

"I have to tell you that bringing all this out into the open is not the easiest thing for me. I appreciate your being so honest about your viewpoint. I hope I can be just as clear about what worries me here."

Or:

"I don't mind telling you that I've got butterflies in my stomach just starting to talk about this. But you've done such a good job of explaining yourself that I feel like I can risk telling the whole

truth as I see it. Let me start with what's been hardest for me lately."

4. Ask for restatements of your position—and corrections of any factual inaccuracies—as necessary. This is the most awkward step of Phase 2, the step that will feel most unnatural and contrived the first few times you attempt it. It may sometimes be unnecessary in relatively smooth negotiations, particularly with people you know well. But asking for a restatement of your position can make a crucial difference in difficult communications with new acquaintances or strangers, or in delicate conversations with anyone close to you. It can also be particularly helpful in business situations where emotional energy has unexpectedly become involved in otherwise "rational" negotiations.

In Phase 1, you repeated the other person's position and asked for confirmations of your understanding. Now in Phase 2, you're simply turning the tables and asking for the same service in return. After you have stated a significant portion of your position, you can invite feedback by asking:

"Would you mind reviewing for me what you've heard me say so far? I'm not sure I'm expressing myself clearly, and it will help me to hear your feedback at this point."

Or:

"Am I making any sense so far? If you wouldn't mind, I'd really appreciate hearing how you'd express what I've said so far. And if I've got any of the facts wrong, please let me know."

Or:

"Please be fair. I proved to you that I thoroughly understood what you were saying. Won't you summarize what I've said just

to be certain I've been as clear about my position as you were about yours?"

You may find the feedback to this request startling. Nine times out of ten, people will not be able to summarize your position very well, or at all—either because they haven't been listening intently enough or because they're inwardly arguing with you even as you speak. Calling for a "sound check" in this fashion reminds both of you of your common goals of respect, understanding, caring, and fairness, and reiterates to your listener that you deserve as much attention and effort as you afforded him or her when you were the listener.

Asking for correction on points of fact establishes that you're not rigidly attached to your way of looking at reality, and that you may not have all the correct or relevant information at hand. Sometimes, however, you may have to reiterate that your *feelings* cannot be corrected. However unreasonable they may be sometimes, your feelings carry messages from your inner spirit that must be decoded and used constructively. If someone begins to tell you your feelings are wrong or inappropriate, you will need to answer back with:

"I can see that you have a difficult time understanding how I can feel the way I do. I'm not defending how I feel. But I'm afraid I have to maintain my right to express whatever I feel, regardless of whether my feelings seem to be out of line with the facts of the situation."

Or:

"I'm willing to look into this further/sleep on it/see if our discussion changes my feelings in the long run, but for now I have to be truthful about what I feel."

Or:

"Whoa, wait a minute! I appreciate the information, but that

doesn't change how I feel about . . . Rather than you telling me what I shouldn't be feeling, I'd really like to hear how you'd express what I am feeling—even if you think it's crazy. Would you mind trying that for me?"

Or:

"Sorry—I guess I'm not up to date. You're absolutely right about . . . , but that doesn't really change my feelings on the situation. Let me see if I can explain why, and then I'd like to hear how it sounds to you, if you don't mind giving me some feedback."

For many people, standing up for their own feelings while admitting errors in perception, gaps in their knowledge, or the very strangeness of those same feelings, can be a daunting challenge. The difficulty is directly proportional to the damage done to their self-esteem in childhood—damage that cannot be repaired by merely trying to appease others. Rather, the inner self needs the outer self to be a brave advocate dedicated to giving and receiving respect, understanding, caring, and fairness. Unless this internal relationship is given the highest priority, all other relationships will be experienced as unrewarding, and conflicts will be looked upon as emotional minefields rather than opportunities for self-discovery.

The dedication to self-respect implied by Ethical Persuasion creates the imperative to speak up on behalf of one's own feelings. The explaining phase of EP is one of advocacy for your inner self, your greatest resource.

5. Review your respective positions. This step may actually be required a number of times during Phase 2, and tends to occur naturally as an outgrowth of the previous step. The fact is that it takes a lot of talking back and forth just for people to understand each other, let alone to solve specific problems. Thus, it's critical to keep checking back all along the way to mutual understanding, and bring this checking to a clear conclusion before proceeding to Phase 3 of Ethical Persuasion. The language can be simple:

"Let's summarize each other's point of view before we begin to look for a solution we can both live with."

Or:

"Thanks for hearing me out so completely. Can we do a brief rundown on both our viewpoints before we move on? I'll review your side and then you can give mine."

Or:

"I feel like I've given this my best shot, and I appreciate your cooperation in confirming your understanding of what I have to say. Unless you have something new to offer, can we make one more translation of each other's viewpoint? I think that'll give us the best possible jumping-off point for what we need to plan / take to the other people involved / work on next."

Note that summarizing *each other's* position is specified here, not delivering a final grand summation of your self-defense (or your blistering prosecution of the "opposition"!).

Typical Difficulties of Phase 2

The three chief resistances that people generally experience along the way to explaining their viewpoint are quite natural. They should neither be denied nor clung to, but simply faced for what they are and examined for what they can teach you about yourself.

First among them is the *fear that revealing your point of view increases your vulnerability*. The answer to this anxiety is, "It certainly does!" But as pointed out earlier, vulnerability gives us strength when we acknowledge its existence to each other and commit to caring for it. Discussing your vulnerability in an intimate relationship is different than in a business or family context. It is necessary to distinguish emotional vulnerability, for instance, from financial or other material forms. But one ground rule remains the same: it is almost always better to risk revealing your vulnerability than to hide or defend it.

The specific end result of this stance is seldom predictable, except to say that it generally offers rewards greater than one can imagine from a position of self-defense. The sharing of vulnerability creates greater bonding and intimacy and is one important step toward achieving greater creativity in problem-solving. Anyone who can consistently lead the way toward this kind of sharing is likely to be recognized as creative and courageous—because he or she has learned to construct or catalyze social environments that promote bonding and cooperation.

A related difficulty has to do with the more popular understanding of vulnerability: the *fear that your point of view will sound unreasonable, silly, weak, or confused.* In dealing with this fear one must be committed to Ethical Persuasion as a self-discovery process that fosters continual personal growth. While stating and exploring your position, it's quite possible that you might have to face the realization that you're "all wrong" about something. However, it's critical to learn to distinguish between being misguided in one's beliefs, attitudes, and feelings, and being intrinsically inadequate or "bad." Paradoxical as it sounds, the more you are open to being mistaken, the better you will come to feel about your strength and intrinsic value. You will also be better prepared to learn from your errors and misperceptions.

Finally, the explaining phase of EP can induce a *fear of*

upsetting the status quo in a relationship. Many long-standing but dysfunctional relationships derive their stability from a significant and fiercely protected degree of misunderstanding and mutual mistreatment. For instance, many families with a substance-abusing parent allow the addict to "act out" in various harmful or even violent ways while the other spouse or children take on "clean-up" roles of codependent responsibility. Someone used to playing the passive caretaker in this kind of situation may be much more afraid to bring out and state their real feelings—of resentment, powerlessness, and shame—than to keep listening attentively to the person who's always been getting most of the attention.

Complicity in one's own abuse at the hands of another is sometimes suffered for the sake of preserving social appearances, or because requiring that one be treated with care and fairness is an unfamiliar and seemingly risky behavior. Less dramatic situations can have lesser degrees of the same kind of complicity, as in the example of a valuable but underpaid employee who's afraid to demand compensation for her real value to her firm because job security looms larger in her mind than the need for self-respect.

Following Courage into Change

The antidote for the preceding fears should sound familiar by now: courage. But courage is not a finite energy bestowed at birth that one must bring forth to *fight off* fears; rather, it is a flexible and growing capacity for change that *uses fears for fuel.* In relationships, courage takes us beyond our familiar limits and into new realms of understanding, where we can keep changing together for the better.

In the previous chapter, I recounted part of an EP counseling session with Jay and Amelia, who were exploring their difficulty in talking openly about the behavior of Jay's mother at family gatherings. I had helped Jay see that admitting he *understood* Amelia's hurt feelings about the situation would not compel him to "take sides" or get involved in the conflict himself. He had further recognized that Amelia had been perceiving him as remote and un-caring because of his evasive behavior. With this much established, Jay was ready to wind up the first phase of Ethical Persuasion on his own.

"Okay, Tom, let me try it," he volunteered. "Amelia, your feeling is that I duck things not just when my mom is around, but even when you and I are discussing her in private. When the going gets tough and you need under-standing, it seems that I'm not loyal or caring about you and the kids. Either I care more about my mom, or I don't care about anyone—these are the feelings I'm getting from you. Is that right?"

"Yes, Jay," Amelia replied quietly. "I'm afraid so."

Jay sighed and sank back in his chair. What he would say next would reveal the leap of understanding he had accomplished—a leap away from the preoccupation with his own self-defense. "Good Lord!" he exclaimed. "If that's the way I come across, I'm amazed you stayed with me this long. No wonder you're so exasperated."

Jay met his wife's eyes for a moment, but he obviously felt too embarrassed to return her small, tentative smile. Perhaps for the first time, he had really entered Amelia's world, and the experience was already beginning to rear-range his own perceptions. Only at this point could Jay proceed with Phase 2 of EP: relating his own viewpoint and feelings. When he glanced at me for guidance, I nodded a go-ahead. He was doing beautifully.

"All right. Let me see if I can take a few minutes to explain myself. I'm not saying I'm right about anything, Amelia, but I do need you to hear what's been going on inside me. And I'm talking about my experience *before* I just listened to you today, because you've given me some things to think about." Acknowledging that he needed time to process material he had just heard during Phase 1 of EP was a wise move on Jay's part. It confirmed that Amelia's revelations really taught him something and that their impasse was already beginning to soften.

"Look, I see how I come across to you now," Jay continued, "but I hope you can understand that, for me, the whole situation with you and my mom is overwhelming. I don't have the words like you do for feelings and it's more than I can handle. I'd rather pound on my thumb with a hammer than be in the room when you two are arguing! I can't stand being around when either one of you is upset, but the combination is just too much. Then when we're alone and you start criticizing me—which feels like an attack, I must admit—I feel like I either have to defend myself or run away. It doesn't seem like there's any other choice; I guess it feels like my survival is at stake and I'd rather be anywhere else."

This all came out in a breathless rush from Jay, who was probably unused to admitting this much vulnerability. Trying to be helpful, Amelia jumped to an inaccurate conclusion: "So what you're saying is that you just don't like to deal with feelings?"

Jay shook his head, looking a little lost. "No, no, that's not quite it. Let me try again. What I'm saying is . . . for some reason, it's tremendously upsetting for me to be around you and Mom when you're upset. I have more feelings than I know what to do with, honey. If I knew how, I'd try to make everything okay for both of you—I feel like I *should* be able to do that—but I don't know the answer, so I go into some kind of shutdown. I just have to get away."

Amelia began to look a little puzzled by this statement from Jay, and a few more attempts at restating his viewpoint were required from her before they came close to a mutual understanding. I offered both of them my opinion that a man's sensitivity to the feelings of his wife or lover may be rooted in an ancient fear of losing the support of his mother, the primary caregiver in childhood. By contrast, a woman's sensitivity to her mate's feelings is *not* rooted in the fear of losing her primary caregiver. For obvious reasons, her partner's maleness does not trigger that kind of anxiety. Furthermore, it's easier for her to model herself on her mother's supportive nature, and so she carries less anxiety about "losing Mother" into her adult life than a man does. However, many women do experience an emotional distance from their fathers—a distance they may still be trying to close with their intimate male partners. But because women are so much better at expressing their feelings when they arise, the depth of men's feelings often go unrecognized by everyone (unless and until they erupt in violence, in many unfortunate cases).

Near the end of their session, Amelia seemed transfixed by what she had learned about Jay's inner experience. "I guess what you're saying is that you have feelings about this situation that may be even more intense than mine," she remarked to her husband. "That's going to take some getting used to, because your actions always suggest the exact opposite. It's definitely going to change my way of thinking about us, because I'm used to perceiving you as insensitive."

Having reached this new meeting place of understanding, Jay and Amelia were content to end their session without a particular strategy for handling the next conflict with his mother. They both needed some time to let what they had shared settle in, and see where their new level of mutual understanding would lead them. They were beginning to learn firsthand yet another definition of courage: an unconventional open-mindedness about our potentials as individuals, intimates, and working partners. Courage flows from the decision to go for self-respect, intimacy, and creative brilliance—while all around us shame, alienation, and imitative dullness are so heavily advertised, cheaply available, and certified for safety.

6

Phase 3:
Creating Resolutions

Most of the popular books about negotiating have focused on solving problems and forging practical agreements in relationships, and some of these guides are quite useful. But I believe this book is the first ever to offer a step-by-step technique to achieve *understanding,* which has three important aspects. First, the deeper the understanding you have of yourself, the greater will be the energy, confidence, and authentic personal morality you bring to decision making. Second, the deeper the understanding you have with anyone else, the greater will be the creativity and flexibility the two (or more) of you will enjoy along the way to problem solving. Finally, the more each person *feels* understood, the greater the resonance between you, which will inspire increased cooperation and stability in the relationship.

Thus, the deeper the understanding you can develop

during the first two phases of Ethical Persuasion, the more likely the final phase is to take care of itself. Practical solutions may become obvious to everyone involved without having to be formally pursued. When solutions are not immediately obvious, the following steps will provide a practical framework for creating them.

The Three Steps (Plus Options) of Creating Resolutions

1. Affirm your mutual understanding and confirm that you are both ready to consider options for resolution.
2. Brainstorm multiple options.
3. If a mutually agreeable solution is not yet obvious, try one or more of the following options.
    *   Take time out to reconsider, consult, exchange proposals, and reconvene.
    *   Agree to neutral arbitration, mediation, or counseling.
    *   Compromise between alternate solutions.
    *   Take turns between alternate solutions.
    *   Yield (for now) once your position is thoroughly and respectfully considered.
    *   Assert your positional power after thoroughly and respectfully considering their position.
    *   Agree to disagree and still respect each other; then, if you can, go your separate ways on the particular issue.

1. Affirm your mutual understanding and confirm that you are both ready to consider options for resolution. The last step of Phase 2 required restating each other's viewpoint to confirm mutual understanding. If this has not already led to an obvious, mutually agreeable solution to the problem(s) at hand, then you can lead the discussion into Phase 3 with an affirmation of the important and profound work that has been accomplished so far. You may put it like this:

"Well, I'm proud of both of us. It's not often that people get this far in understanding each other, and that's something we can pat each other on the back for. I think we have a head start on settling the matter of . . . Are you ready to talk about solutions?"

Or:

"Thanks for hanging in there with me long enough for us to reach this understanding. It's clear that we each know where the other's coming from. I'm ready to look at our options now; how about you?"

Or:

"You know, this has been tough but I think we're way ahead of where we started. I'm glad we didn't rush into making a decision before both of us were ready. How about taking a break for a couple hours/a few days/a week before we decide exactly what needs to be done here?"

The last option addresses the possibility of taking a break from the EP process. A time-out may be called for a variety of reasons: the process of reaching and confirming understanding has been particularly stressful; one or both parties has become aware of a significant amount of new information requiring digestion and analysis; or the understanding reached is too unpleasant for either party to continue talking at the moment.

If the prior relationship has owed some of its stability

to long-sustained deception or withholding between people, then the airing-out of repressed feelings that is likely to occur in Phase 1 or 2 may be temporarily destabilizing to the relationship and difficult for people to accept. As it happened for Jay and Amelia in the last chapter, established perceptions and ways of relating can be shaken up and changed forever. It's wise to allow sufficient time for re-orientation and the "decompression" of strong feelings. You can always ask for a break on behalf of yourself or the other person:

"Now that we understand each other, I realize that my whole view of this problem has been a little off / pretty out of whack / completely wrong. I can't be sure of how to proceed until my feelings about the situation are more stable. Can you give me a little time to sort things out?"

Or:

"I really appreciate how hard it's been for you to hear what I had to say; there were some things that were just too uncomfortable to admit before now. I know this will change our relationship down the line, and I'm more interested in long-term closeness than short-term problem solving. If you want to take some time to sort things out, I'm happy to put off any decision about what to do about . . . for a little while."

2. Brainstorm multiple options. If you remain focused on end results instead of the process of understanding, you won't get very far in the first two phases of EP. But even after confirming mutual understanding, you may still retain a pet theory about what should be done to resolve a specific conflict. This is the time, however, to throw open the doors and windows, mentally speaking, and allow the greatest possible range of creative ideas to be voiced and discussed. You don't have to discard your theory, but you do need to be ready for the possibility that another person has an even more brilliant approach, or that one will emerge during mutual brainstorming. The more playful you can make this process, the better. You can lead the way with suggestions like:

"I have some ideas about what we can do next, but I'm curious to hear if anything has occurred to you in the way of solutions. Let's exchange ideas."

Or:

"Now that we know what our issues are, I think we have a good foundation for working this out together. I'm ready to look at anything you'd like to put on the table."

Or:

"Can we spend some time tossing around possible alternatives for resolving this situation? Let's not worry about practicality for the moment. I'd like to come up with as many ideas as we can right now and sort out the best ones later."

3. If a mutually agreeable solution is not yet obvious, try one or more of the following options.

Take time out to reconsider, consult, exchange proposals, and reconvene. Here's another opportunity to take time out during EP; I believe there can't be too many. This option is particularly relevant to decision making that involves a number of people, as in business situations in which two or a few are representing many others. But even intimate partners may want to talk over their feelings and their imminent decisions with friends or counselors outside the relationship that's being worked on. Depending on the situation, you can approach this step by saying:

"Well, I feel like we have a number of ways we can go now.

Let me talk to my boss/my co-workers/my staff and see how these ideas we've discussed go over. If there's anyone you want to consult, feel free."

Or:

"I like the possibilities we've both laid out here, but I'm not quite ready to choose one over the other. Can I get back to you in a little while?"

Or:

"I feel like we're very close to a solution now, but I'd really like to talk to my best friend/counselor/sister/brother/parents about what's in front of us. If you want to talk it over with someone important to you, I'd appreciate hearing their opinion, too. Can we take a little time out for that?"

Or:

"I'd like to back off from this overnight and sleep on it. Perhaps I'll think and feel differently tomorrow."

Agree to neutral arbitration, mediation, or counseling. In some situations, you may want to introduce the idea of inviting an outside consultant into your decision-making process—either because someone has a particular expertise you can both make use of or because feelings remain too intense at the moment for one or both parties to allow possible solutions to be rationally discussed. Possible openings include:

"The ideas we have on the table now look good to me, but I think we could benefit from some outside expertise. Are you open to inviting a consultant into our next discussion?"

Or:

"I think we understand each other now, and the lines are pretty clearly drawn about our different approaches to a solution. I think a mediator could help us bridge the gap and save time/ avoid litigation/come up with a compromise we haven't thought

of. Do you have any recommendations? / Are you willing to consider someone I can recommend?"

Or:

"I understand that your feelings are still hurt over some of the things I said / I'm still pretty upset about what we've learned about each other. We may not be able to settle on our next step until we bring in a counselor. I'd be happy to consider anyone you could recommend. / Are you willing to consider someone I have in mind?"

Keep in mind that any suggestion you have about the course of Phase 3 should follow the structure of what has occurred before in EP: ask for the other person's viewpoint before proceeding with any concrete action. Don't hire a mediator or counselor without consulting the other person first, and whenever possible, ask for references from potential advisers.

If the other person has some resistance to consultation, return to Phase 1 to gain an understanding of that resistance *before* stating all your reasons for pursuing outside assistance. The rule of thumb is: *Resistance increases under pressure, and dissolves when respectfully and considerately explored.* Following this rule can make all the difference between the other person actively resisting the help you might bring in against their will, and the other person being willing to listen to consultation despite their acknowledged feelings of resistance.

Compromise between alternate solutions. What Ethical Persuasion brings to the age-old art of compromise is a deeper and broader understanding of the situation between people in negotiation, encompassing not just their rational viewpoints but their feelings as well. EP encourages compromises that serve the long-term health of relationships and the vitality of the values of respect, understanding, caring, and fairness.

When a compromise between alternate solutions seems possible, it's very useful to acknowledge once again that you're looking beyond short-term answers. You might say:

"It looks like we can both give a little and come up with a workable compromise here. But let's make sure that we're coming up with something that we both feel as good as we can about, given the circumstances, and that keeps our mutual respect intact. It would be a shame to waste all this work we've done together on a sloppy deal."

Or:

"Look, I'm ready to do . . . if you're ready to do . . . Does that feel good to you? Do you think it will hold up for a while?"

Or:

"What our counselor/mediator has suggested as a compromise will work for me. Can you think it over and let me know how you feel? We can always check on things later and revise as necessary, but I'd like to know for sure that this solution seems fair and respectful to you."

Take turns between alternate solutions. Sometimes the health of a relationship will best be maintained by taking turns with unpleasant tasks or decisions about minor choices. Imagine, for instance, a large family that is used to having a housekeeper has to cut costs to keep its budget in line. Using Ethical Persuasion, the parents could explain the full situation to their kids and solicit their ideas on how household tasks could be shared and rotated fairly. Or a couple who have had a tendency to fight over who chooses movies or restaurants could decide simply to alternate on who decides for a while: first one and then the other could set their joint agenda without having to hear or discuss objections. Over the long term, of course, it's probably better for such a couple to learn to make mutually enjoyable choices. But taking turns can be a positive interim step toward long-term improvement of any kind of relationship. The proposition can be quite simple:

"Okay, you want to do this and I want to do that. Maybe we should just take turns for a while and see where that leads us."

Or:

"Look, we both understand now what's been going on in this power struggle of ours. Neither one of us is right or wrong; we just like different things and we want to do them together. Maybe we can just take turns until a better way becomes clear to us."

Or:

"I understand now that we've been doing mostly what I want because I'm the boss/father/mother and you've been afraid to speak up. But I respect your ideas/what you need to do/your right to have your way, so let's do it your way for a little while. We'll see what happens."

Yield (for now) once your position is thoroughly and respectfully considered. This solution is less than optimal, but preferable over a hostile break in communications. I'm convinced that full understanding between people always leads to workable (and sometimes even miraculous) solutions, but such happy endings may not result immediately. When anyone's hurt or when angry feelings are persisting long past the listening and explaining phases, you may be faced with making a choice between going your own way alone toward what you think is a good solution or letting the other person have their way for the time being. The latter is usually the wisest choice if you are in a subordinate position in an organization.

From the EP viewpoint, yielding is not just a matter of backing down because the heat is too intense or someone has positional power over you. Even as you retreat, you can remind the other person that you appreciate the degree of understanding that has been reached so far and that you are yielding because it's the practical thing to do at the moment out of respect for their position, or to preserve the relationship. That's the exercise of personal power. It's easier if you're the one having less intense feelings, but it's not impossible if things are the other way around. You can say:

"This has been very tough for me so far and I'm not happy with what I've heard. But I think you're being honest with me and I respect that. My feelings about this are just too strong for me to be certain that I'm right, so I'm going to follow your lead on this matter. But I want to make sure that we can check back soon to see if this solution is really working well."

Or:

"I feel very strongly that my solution to this problem is a good one, but it's not worth forcing it on you if our relationship is damaged in the long run. I'm going to back off for now, but you can be sure I'll keep working on it in my mind. Maybe when things have calmed down a little we can strike a better bargain."

Or:

"I really appreciate the time you've taken to explain yourself/your position as manager/the company's viewpoint to me, and to understand my point of view. I have a better understanding of the whole situation than when we started, although that doesn't change my idea about what I deserve/what I'd like to see changed/what I should be doing next. But I'm willing to hold off on my want list until we can agree that it's workable. Can we talk this over again in a month/six months/a year?"

Or:

"I'm really struck by the courage you've shown in coming out and telling me exactly what you feel. I know it's very difficult for you in this situation, and you've made it clear that you feel very uncomfortable with my suggestion about the next step we should take. So I'm willing to hold off on that for a while / leave things the way they are for now / take your suggestion instead. Let's talk again soon and see how we're both feeling about the future."

Assert your positional power after thoroughly and respect- fully considering their position. If you have positional power in your job or family, you may sometimes have to make decisions that affect other people before a mutual agreement about what to do can be reached. Let's say, for instance, that you are a small-business owner who has been approached by an employee about getting a raise. After thoroughly sounding him out using Ethical Persuasion and reaching a solid understanding of each other's position, the decision of whether or not to grant the raise is still up to you. You've honestly told your employee that you need a few days to think the matter over. Your employee is anxious, however, and wants to know your decision right away—on a Friday afternoon, before he goes home for the weekend.

At this point, the EP approach to resolving the dilemma would be to remind your employee that you have proven to *his* satisfaction that you understand his position and his anxiety: "I know this is important to you, and of course you'd like to go home and tell your wife that the raise is coming through. But as I said earlier, I need a little time to look at the books and see if I can afford this right now. I promise that I'll have an answer for you Monday."

But your employee keeps on the pressure, saying that

he doesn't want to live with uncertainty about the raise over the weekend. While you certainly could pursue ever deeper understanding with him, there are other things you need to do. It's not practical to continue the discussion at the moment, and you do need time to mull it over. That means you must resort to ethical use of your positional power: "Look, we've agreed that you've gotten a fair hearing on this issue, and I think you understand why I don't want to say yes on the spot. Now we both need to get back to work and wrap things up for the week. But if you can't live with the uncertainty and you absolutely must have an answer now, then the answer is no. If you can wait till Monday, the answer might be yes. I can't promise that, but your chances are better if you give me the time to think it over."

This example demonstrates the fact that ethical decision making is not synonymous with weakness or waffling on the issues. Some people in positions of authority may fear having too much understanding of other people's viewpoints because it might seem to complicate decision making and influence them to attempt to satisfy everyone's needs when that is practically impossible.

For anyone with positional power, however, the proper use of Ethical Persuasion is to *learn* and *acknowledge* everyone's needs in a particular situation—not to fulfill them all and please everyone, which is often impossible. After recognizing and paying respect to everyone's needs and vulnerability, you must also admit your own vulnerability—at least to yourself—which includes the pain involved in decisions that you know you must make and that you know will probably be imperfect. Acknowledging our limitations while dedicating ourselves to solid efforts based on ethical values is sometimes the best we have to offer.

For the people influenced by your decisions, admitting this vulnerability will distinguish you from the type of authority figures who wield power without apparent concern for the human consequences. Over the long run, your candor can only increase the respect you receive, thus augmenting your personal power. If you have positional power, your aim should be to make your authority irrelevant, relying on personal power to influence people to participate creatively in making decisions. Thus, your positional power becomes the power of last resort. When absolutely necessary, you can exert it with language like:

"We've talked this over thoroughly, and I appreciate your confirmation that I understand the situation. Now, however, somebody has to make a decision, and that somebody is me. We haven't been able to come to an agreement about the solutions on the table, but our time has run out. Since I have the ultimate responsibility, I'm going to proceed with . . . Let's keep in touch and see how things turn out. I'll appreciate your continuing input."

Or:

"I really appreciate that you've leveled with me and your mother/father about this. It's important to us that we understand what you're feeling, and we wanted you to know how things are for us, too. This is one of those times when we have the responsibility to decide what's best all around, even though you want to do something else for yourself. When you're out on your own, you can go right ahead. But we still pay the bills for the household, and we just can't afford this/don't think it's right/ don't think you're ready. It hurts us to disappoint you, but that's the best we can do right now. We're not saying that we know

*for certain we're right, and we won't blame you if you're angry
with us right now. We also want to keep the lines open about
this, so let's talk again in a couple weeks and see how everybody
feels."*

**Agree to disagree and still respect each other; then, if you
can, go your separate ways on the particular issue.** In conflicts in which no particular decision is required of anyone
and mutual understanding has brought people to the point
of merely acknowledging how differently they see things,
there may occasionally be nothing left to do but part ways,
temporarily or permanently, on peaceful terms. Still, it's
worth acknowledging that Ethical Persuasion has brought
everyone closer through the exercise of respect, understanding, caring, and fairness, even if agreement and resolution are not yet in sight. It's also important to affirm
the potential for future progress. You might put it like
this:

*"I guess we're not getting any further with this for the time
being. I'm sorry that we couldn't settle things / part on friendlier
terms / come up with an answer that satisfies everyone, but I think
we came a long way from where we started by confirming our
understanding of each other. Perhaps we should just give ourselves
some time to think things over and give it another try later. Does
that seem reasonable to you?"*

Or:

*"It's clear that we come from very different worlds. Maybe
we'll never reach a mutual conclusion about this, but I'm proud
that we've talked this over in an atmosphere of respect and fairness. That's quite an accomplishment in itself. I wish you the
best in your work, and maybe when our paths cross again we'll
find that we agree about more than we used to."*

Or:

"I guess we're not going to work this out. That hurts me because we've been close for a long time, but at least our differences are clear now. I may not agree with what you want to do with your life, but I respect your right to go your own way. I also appreciate your honesty, and I've tried to do just as well on that score. I won't forget what we've meant to each other; I hope you won't, either. If you're agreeable, I'd like to keep in touch."

The Willingness to Change

An attitude that can greatly enhance your problem-solving capacity in the final phase of Ethical Persuasion is expressed by the question "What change can I make?" This is absolutely the best perspective to apply to any moment of decision and choice in a relationship; you can increase your power by making clear your willingness to take responsible action to change things and improve the situation at hand. Willingness to change, however, does not imply that you are at fault for any existing problem—merely that you are ready to take responsibility for improving the relationship.

I learned this one day when I noticed that my wife, Judy, seemed irritated with me, but I did not know why. When I was younger, I would have either ignored her behavior and retaliated with prolonged sullenness or confronted her with a declaration like "I can't stand you being so irritable!" This time, however, I initiated a shorthand form of EP by saying, "I get the feeling that I'm very irritating to you today, and I just can't stand being seen by you as irritating. Is there something I can do to change this?" This successfully opened the door to a discussion of some feelings within and between us that had gone too long unrecognized. Discussion eventually erased the irritation of the moment and deepened our relationship.

Notice that I did not confess to *being* an irritating person when I didn't think I was one—merely that I could tell Judy was seeing me that way. I couldn't force her to change her point of view, but I could express my desire not to be seen that way—and back up that desire by stating my willingness to start the ball rolling for change. By the way, I did learn why Judy was hurt and angry, and part of the reason turned out to be problems of her own that had nothing to do with me. She had not examined her own discomfort until I offered to become less irritating to her; thus we both learned and benefited as a result of my willingness to change.

However difficult it is to change oneself—and it can be a full-time challenge—it is infinitely harder to force change in another person. In any relationship difficulty, it's more powerful to take responsibility for changing your own attitudes and actions simply because it's smarter and more likely to succeed. It also sets an example that influences other people far more effectively than any kind of blame, intimidation, or manipulation you could devise.

Learning EP in Bits and Pieces

I've presented the technique of Ethical Persuasion in this part of the book in orderly phases, steps, and options because that's the best way to learn it in book form. In the real world, of course, your conversations and your self-training will not be nearly so orderly. Listening to someone explain their viewpoint will often overlap with explaining your own viewpoint, and resolutions to particular problems may pop up before you feel like real understanding has been reached. There's nothing to stop you from pursuing further understanding in such a case, but other people who are heavily solution-oriented may want to move on at that moment. You can always express your interest in continuing to work for greater understanding after a particular problem has been resolved.

An Ethical Persuasion process may have to be stretched over a few or many encounters, or it may occasionally seem to complete itself with exceptional rapidity. I've also had the experience of offering to hear out someone's hostile viewpoint in depth, only to have them simply go away without any explanation—as if they were primarily interested in the opportunity for conflict. Sometimes a person who only wants to do battle is stunned by the offer of respectful negotiations.

As you begin to practice EP, you are likely to find that you are better at some parts of it than others. Perhaps it comes naturally to you to respect and acknowledge the feelings that all sides bring to a negotiation, yet it feels too awkward at first to restate another person's feelings in your own words. Or you may excel in affirming and confirming another person's thoughts and feelings, but feel tongue-tied and threatened when it's your turn to reveal yourself.

Whatever the difficulty, try to remember that Ethical Persuasion is a process of ongoing self-discovery and the improvement of relationships—not a technique that can be entirely mastered through memorization and one or two rehearsals. Role-playing can certainly help you learn to use EP, but the best way is to apply the most understanding you have at any moment to a real-life conversation. Later, you can review how well you did at each phase and decide what aspects you need to improve. With practice, the bits and pieces of EP that you have mastered will come together into a communicating style that seems much greater than the sum of its parts, just the way that the incomprehensible phrases of a foreign language eventually come together in your mind to form a whole new perspective and natural way of speaking.

Five Points to Remember

In brief, the most important points about the three phases of Ethical Persuasion are as follows:

1. Remember and respect *the presence of feelings* in all high-energy communications.
2. Make it clear that *problem solving can wait until full, mutual understanding* is achieved and confirmed. State clearly and reiterate often that you are not interested in defending yourself or criticizing others. Your primary goals are *respect, understanding, caring, and fairness*—the qualities that guarantee the health of long-term relationships.
3. To maximize your personal power, offer to *listen to the other person's viewpoint first* and explain yours later.
4. To confirm mutual understanding, *restate the other person's viewpoint in your own words* and ask whether you've got it right. Later, ask the other person to do the same for you.
5. Remember that the best way to improve a relationship is to *change yourself* in a positive direction.

Part III

Applying Ethical Persuasion

This part of the book will help you see how the phases and steps of EP can be applied and adapted to real-life situations in three different arenas: intimate relationships (Chapter 7), the workplace (Chapter 8), and the family (Chapter 9). Each of these chapters begins with a rerouting of one of the failed dialogues from Chapter 1. Finally, the last chapter outlines some of the possible approaches you can take in exceptionally difficult situations where Ethical Persuasion may seem practically impossible.

Some of these chapters may seem to be of less immediate interest to you than others, but useful suggestions for the general application of EP appear in all of them. You'll also find a number of provocative ideas about the broader philosophical implications of EP—for instance, how it can provide the basis for a whole new approach to child-rearing, briefly outlined in Chapter 9. As suggested in the concluding epilogue, Ethical Persuasion creates a new meeting ground for personal and social change. Using it to improve your immediate relationships will have a positive effect on the larger world around you.

7

Friends, Lovers, and Spouses

Now that you've learned the basics of Ethical Persuasion, let's take a look at how it might work in the context of intimate relationships. What follows is a "rerouting" of the first dialogue from Chapter 1, in which Gail and Perry found themselves in a heated discussion over issues of commitment and fairness. This time the same dialogue will be altered by Perry's introduction of the EP process, at a point after the basic issues of their conflict have been established—and when Perry becomes aware of the strong feelings that are present on both sides of the conversation.

Pay special attention to Perry's patience in eliciting Gail's true feelings about the situation. He provides an excellent example of the fulfillment of Phase 1 of Ethical Persuasion.

Control vs. Commitment: Working It Out Together

PERRY: Hi, honey. You certainly sound like you're in a good mood.

GAIL: [*Chuckling*] Well, I was just going through my clothes for our trip when you called, and when the phone rang I just knew it was you. Do you want me to go through your closet, too?

PERRY: [*Laughing uneasily*] Well, I guess you know me pretty well by now—wardrobe is not my strong point. If I had five copies of my gray suit for the office, I'd be set for life. . . . But I *am* calling about the trip, honey. A little problem has come up.

GAIL: What kind of problem?

PERRY: Well, you remember that I had this weekend open because the kids were supposed to go see their cousins?

GAIL: They were going to stay with your sister Charlotte.

PERRY: Right. Well, her kids are both coming down with the flu or something. Anyway, nobody's having any fun over there, so the big reunion of the cousins is off. . . . So, uh, it's still my turn with the kids.

GAIL: What do you mean, Perry?

PERRY: I mean they have to be with me for the long weekend. It would have been my turn anyway except that they—

GAIL: But Perry, we've had this planned for weeks! Can't Sharon take care of them?

PERRY: Well, honey, you know Sharon and I have this visitation agreement, and she made plans, too. I hate to ask her to change her plans around when it's not her turn.

GAIL: But did you?

PERRY: Did I what?

GAIL: Did you ask Sharon if she could change her plans?

PERRY: No, not exactly. I told her you and I were really looking forward to this trip, but you know . . . it's just not her concern. I mean, I have to be fair.

GAIL: Well, how about being fair to me? Don't I get some consideration? I'm getting a little tired of the feeling that you just squeeze me in when it's no trouble for Sharon or the kids.

[*At this point, the dialogue diverges from its course in Chapter 1, as Perry recognizes the emergence of strong feelings in the conversation and initiates the first phase of Ethical Persuasion.*]

PERRY: Honey, what are you saying? You're obviously upset, and I don't blame you. I'm upset, too. But let me see if I understand you: Are you feeling that I care less about you than I do about Sharon and the kids? Is that what you're saying?

GAIL: Of course that's what I'm saying! This isn't the first time that Sharon and the kids came first, no matter how it affected our plans. I think there's a pretty clear pattern here.

PERRY: Okay, okay—you've got a point. But let me make absolutely certain that I understand. What you're saying is that I have never, ever asked Sharon to compromise for the sake of you and me, and that it seems like I'd rather disappoint you than run the risk of upsetting Sharon. Is that what you think?

GAIL: Yes, it is—because it's true!

PERRY: Well, if that's the way you see it, then I can understand why you're so upset. That would make sense —how else could it look to you? It must look like I just don't care about you that much—and I just hate that you're getting that impression, because it isn't true. That's not how *I* feel. I don't blame you for it, but I hate that it comes across that way, and that you're hurt because of it.

GAIL: Really, Perry? Are you just saying that, or do you really understand?

PERRY: From the way you're asking that, I guess I've made it hard for you to believe that I can understand your feelings, Gail. You're obviously skeptical; I must have been giving you lots of reasons to think I don't care about your feelings when push comes to shove. How can I convince you that right at this moment I'm very sorry about the way things look to you? Because it's just not true that I care less about you than Sharon.

GAIL: Well, Perry, I guess I need to see some real evidence of the pattern changing before I'll believe it. At least I can see now that you're *trying* to understand. . . . By the way, it's not too late to ask Sharon if she can take care of the kids this weekend, you know.

[*Perry has now come to an understanding of Gail's position, and verified his understanding with her. She has just suggested a resolution that Perry is willing to consider, but before they decide on it, he wants to make sure that Gail understands* him—*Phase 2 of Ethical Persuasion.*]

PERRY: That's true. I can do that, although I can't make any promises about what she'll say. But before I ask her, I need to make some things clear about what I'm feeling. Now that I have a better understanding of how *you* see things, I want to make sure that you understand

where I'm really coming from. Does that sound fair
to you?

GAIL: [*Cautiously*] Of course, Perry.

PERRY: Okay. I can understand that it looks like I must care
less about you than about Sharon and the kids. I don't
blame you for feeling that at all, Gail. But I really do
need to try to explain what I've been feeling, because
it's pretty clear that I haven't been coming across well.
You see, my actual reasons for doing things the way
I've been doing them are not what you think they are.
You think I just don't care much about you—

GAIL: No, that's not quite right, Perry. I know you care
—you just don't care about me *enough* to ever risk putting Sharon out. It's not that you have to hurt her to
prove anything to me; it just seems to me like you
haven't yet made a choice for *our* relationship.

PERRY: Okay. Fair enough. You feel like second fiddle and
you think that's the way I really want things. Have I
got that right?

GAIL: Yes. That's exactly how it feels to me, Perry.

PERRY: Okay, let me try to explain how I've been feeling.
I'm going to have to think out loud here, so please bear
with me. . . .

The thing is, I guess I've been asking you to share in
my difficulties because I *already* see us as partners, and
I want things to go as smoothly as possible. With
Sharon, it's not very smooth sometimes, especially if
she thinks I'm not living up to my side of our visitation
agreement. When any kind of conflict comes up, I try
to handle things in the way that I think will be smoothest
for both you and me.

GAIL: But you never ask *me* about it, Perry. The decision
is made before I get a chance to say anything!

PERRY: Well, you may be right. I guess I'm still in a pattern I had with Sharon. You know, we divorced basically because we could never get over this thing about compromise. In the early days, she would make such a scene about not getting her way that I got into a habit of not bringing things up. I would make whatever decision I thought would keep the peace, and not upset her. Because I paid a very high price whenever I crossed her— and so did the kids, by the way.

Finally, it was just too difficult to discuss anything. We couldn't make the marriage work anymore. And I guess I thought I was getting away from the problem when I got away from the marriage . . . but here I am, still avoiding confrontations with her, and now it's *our* problem. When I think about it, I realize I've always had a hard time bringing up anything difficult with women I care about, starting with my mother. I'm always trying not to rock the boat because I really, really hate to see a woman upset, especially if she's upset with me.

GAIL: But we get upset anyway, don't we? Have you ever thought that maybe we get the most upset when you don't even ask our opinion about important decisions?

PERRY: Well, maybe I'm beginning to see that. I used to think that always giving in was noble; I could give up something and avoid hurting Sharon. But maybe it was also a backward way of taking control. . . . I don't know. Whatever it was, it didn't work. I just feel like I'm between a rock and a hard place now, honey. It's like I've got to upset one or the other of you, and I can't stand it.

GAIL: Well, I guess you have to decide what you really want most right now, Perry. It's not that I want you always giving in to me; I want to know that you care. A big part of it is that we hardly ever talk this way, honey—I didn't know you felt all these pressures. I need to know what's going on with you—that's what a relationship is. It's not just a matter of keeping the peace. . . .

Look, I'm not Sharon *or* your mother. I know I can come on a little strong sometimes, but I'm willing to deal with difficulties that come up, if you tell me about them when they come up and not after you've already decided what to do. It's possible to work things out *together,* you know.

PERRY: I guess so; I'm just not used to being so up-front with my feelings, and it may take me a while to get used to it. I must have made some progress, though, because it's clear that at least you're willing to understand and hear me out. I certainly never had that feeling with Sharon, and I really appreciate the difference, Gail. It takes some of the pressure off. Maybe there's even a way out of this that won't be so terrible. . . .

[*Phase 2 of the EP process is now complete, and Perry is prepared to resume discussion of the resolution suggested earlier by Gail.*]

Look, I need to know that you're with me no matter what happens now. I'll call Sharon and ask her if she can do me a favor this time. It's not something I look forward to, but I'll certainly take it on for our sake, for you and me. I'm just not optimistic about what Sharon will say, because she isn't one to give up her plans. If I have to take the kids this weekend, can you and I still work something out? Will you take a rain check on the bed-and-breakfast?

GAIL: Well, let's take it one step at a time, okay? First let me know what Sharon says. But if she gives you a hard time, please don't keep it all bottled up and tell me everything's fine! Let's see what happens next and then decide what we want to do.

PERRY: [*Laughing*] Okay, sweetie. Boy, this is tough. Thanks for hearing me out; it really changes things.

GAIL: Yeah, I think that's what it's all about. I'll talk to you in a little while. . . . I do love you, you know.

PERRY: I love you, too. I'll let you know what happens.

[*Even though the ultimate resolution to this problem is not clear by the dialogue's end, a much more important goal has been achieved: a greater intimacy and sense of mutual understanding and support between Gail and Perry. Perry has also gained an important insight into his relationship patterns, while making clear to Gail that her initial perception of his motives was not correct. This dialogue illustrates that Ethical Persuasion is a process that puts learning and understanding before any other short-term goals.*]

Reading Between the Lines

Let's take a look at what's going on between the lines of this EP-altered dialogue. When Perry checks out his understanding of Gail's feelings by remarking "What you're saying is that I have never, ever asked Sharon to compromise . . ." he's giving Gail a clue that her position sounds very extreme to him. No doubt Perry feels that Gail is factually incorrect; perhaps he has asked his ex-wife to compromise once or twice (though probably to no avail, which means Gail might not have known). But it would not be fruitful here to try to force Gail to concede the point. Perry's only goal here is to assure Gail that he understands *how she sees the situation*—not to determine whether her view is factually accurate.

Many male-female exchanges get hung up on exactly this kind of issue. A man may try to establish the rational "truth" of a situation in the belief that an objective agreement about "just the facts" will benefit everyone. This typically masculine motive is not just a love of truth; often it also has to do with the avoidance of acknowledging, examining, and expressing feelings. A woman's view of the truth will generally include more of the feelings surrounding the facts, and so she may find a man's version of reality somewhat cold, hard-edged, and uncaring.

A woman in a dispute with a rationalist man is thus likely to sense that her feelings—and by extension, herself—are not even being heard. She is much less likely to be interested in the objective circumstances of the issue being discussed than in the moment-to-moment quality of the relationship. From that perspective, feelings are always relevant facts in themselves. Learning to manage feelings well is critical to teamwork, effective negotiating, and certainly intimacy. That doesn't mean feelings must always be *acted* on or even expressed, because they could indeed lead to error or further misunderstanding. But strong feelings must always be acknowledged and respected, not denied simply because they seem to contradict a supposedly detached version of the truth.

By stating Gail's position in absolute terms ("never, ever") Perry gives her the chance to clarify and soften her stance. Many people would soften up a little when they realize that they are coming across as more extreme than they actually feel. Gail does not soften, however; she wants Perry to know just how hurt she is. She even goes so far as to say that "it's true!" that Perry would rather disappoint her than upset Sharon—when, of course, she doesn't *know* that it's true, only that it feels that way to her.

At this point, Perry might naturally feel tempted to respond "That is *not* true!" in defense of how he actually feels when caught in a classic rock-and-a-hard-place circumstance. But he remembers that the first phase of EP is devoted to giving his partner a full, sincere hearing, and to checking out his understanding of her feelings. So he says instead that "if that's the way you see it, then I can understand why you're so upset."

The damaged condition of their mutual trust is revealed when Gail challenges Perry's first offering of understanding: "Really, Perry? Are you just saying that, or do you really understand?" Again he must resist the temptation to say something like "What do you think I am, a liar?" He demonstrates great skill at being respectful and understanding by accepting Gail's challenge with, "From the way you're asking that, I guess I've made it hard for you to believe that I can understand your feelings . . ."

Giving In—Or Waiting His Turn?

Is Perry giving in too much by not challenging Gail's version of their reality together? No, in fact he is doing something quite valuable and rare in human conflicts: acknowledging that his partner lives in a different world of personal experience, and also that her point of view is justified for anyone living *inside* that world. He would naturally want this much recognition for his own point of view, and so he is fulfilling Phase 1 of EP in order to give Gail a complete hearing.

This provides Perry with the moral leverage to request a fair hearing, after Gail has certified that Perry understands her. She begins to do so ("I can see now that you're *trying* to understand . . ."), but then senses that she might be able to push her preferred resolution into the opening that Perry has provided: "By the way, it's not too late to ask Sharon if she can take care of the kids . . ."

Here Perry must stand up for the right to explain himself before any resolution is pursued (Phase 2 before Phase 3, in EP terms). "Now that I have a better understanding of how *you* see things, I want to make sure that you understand where I'm really coming from. Does that sound fair to you?" he asks. Gail agrees that it does, although it soon becomes clear that Perry's understanding of her is not yet complete. When he skillfully opens up his side of things by referring back to hers ("You think I just don't care much about you"), she has to tell him he hasn't quite got it right. She explains further, then he restates her position: "You feel like second fiddle and you think that's the way I really want things." Again he asks for a Phase 1 confirmation: "Have I got that right?"

"Yes," Gail replies, "that's exactly how it feels to me, Perry."

Now Phase 1 is really fulfilled, and Perry begins to explore the mixture of powerful feelings that have been motivating his failed attempts to make things go smoothly. Like many men, Perry tries to fix conflicts between himself and women by taking emotional shortcuts, a strategy that women tend to perceive as insensitive and controlling. What women often do not see—largely because men work so hard to conceal it, sometimes even from themselves— is how sensitive men are to the upset of any women close to them. "I really, really hate to see a woman upset,"

Perry bravely reveals, "especially if she's upset with me."

As I suggested earlier in this book, I believe this kind of male vulnerability has much to do with a man's tendency to relate emotionally to a woman he cares about as he once did to his mother, the primary care giver during the most vulnerable part of his life. The displeasure of a man's intimate female partner can make him so painfully uncomfortable that he feels unworthy even of *his right to exist*—just as a mother's displeasure would threaten a little boy's sense of security. The adult male's reaction to this extreme and humiliating discomfort is to assert his independence and difference from the female. He may even be openly resentful of her unhappiness because it provokes his feelings of unworthiness.

By contrast, a little girl is less threatened by her father's disapproval as long as she has her mother's support. When she does feel threatened, she reacts by first trying to improve her relatedness to her mother, and later to others. Psychological testing of men and women has revealed that men often fear intimacy as a form of entrapment in which they suspect they will be humiliated or betrayed; women are more likely to fear isolation or abandonment, and seek intimacy to prevent those conditions.

And so I disagree with some popular diagnoses of man/woman communication problems, whenever they assert that men are primarily motivated toward control of their relationships (whereas women are motivated purely toward relatedness). I think a man maneuvers for control of intimate relationships because of a childlike *fear of being overwhelmed* by a woman's discontent, which would remind him of maternal disapproval. Because the typical man in our culture does not have the skills to assuage this fear by explaining (or even recognizing!) his feelings, he resorts to the kind of power maneuverings that the same culture rewards him for using in his professional life.

Perry recognizes this tendency in himself when he admits that his well-meaning manipulations of Gail and Sharon may amount to "a backward way of taking control." Seeing this doesn't let him off the hook emotionally; he ends up feeling like he has to displease one woman or the other, and it's clearly not something he looks forward to. But in opening up to Gail—and gaining considerable insight into himself in the process—he has, by conversation's end, gone a long way toward restoring trust and openness in his current primary relationship.

This can hardly do anything but help Perry to pursue a better relationship with his ex-wife and children, as his fear of relating honestly to women eventually decreases and his load of general anxiety lightens. His self-respect will improve gradually as well, since he will be standing up for his own point of view more clearly and consistently.

Gail has some fears to overcome as well. The conversation reveals that she is exceptionally sensitive to anything she perceives as manipulation, no doubt because she feels that past men in her life have exerted too much control over her. In her resentful tone and her pushing of a preferred resolution there is plentiful evidence that she is no stranger to power plays herself. She sees this about herself in the conversation ("I know I can come on a little strong sometimes . . ."), but she can obviously be Perry's teacher on one very important aspect. "I'm willing to deal with difficulties that come up," she tells him, "if you tell me about them when they come up and not after you've already decided what to do. It's possible to work things out *together,* you know." In that respect, Gail shows a natural understanding of Ethical Persuasion.

Understanding Gender Differences

Over the past fifteen years, countless self-help books have been devoted to the diagnosis of gender differences and "syndromes," without much headway being made in the real quality of communication between women and men. Many of the typical issues were cogently summed up in the runaway best-seller *You Just Don't Understand*, wherein author Deborah Tannen, Ph.D., concluded that the sexes actually speak in different "genderlects" that obscure the real intentions and meanings of men and women as surely as if they were speaking different languages from different cultures.

"Understanding genderlects makes it possible to change—to try speaking differently—when you want to. But even if no one changes, understanding genderlect improves relationship," Tannen asserts near the close of her book. I feel, however, that the mere recognition of gender differences in communication will not improve relationships very much. What will dramatically improve male-female relationships is not simply understanding genderlects, but understanding *each other* as unique beings in any particular encounter. If no one changes, the kind of understanding that can be reached will tend to be minimal, static, and prone to disintegration. *The process of achieving real understanding is a process of change.* Anyone who takes even the most tentative steps into Phase 1 of Ethical Persuasion during a conflicted encounter will rapidly gain a gut-level grasp of what that means.

In the following section I'm going to list and briefly describe a few of the major issues and conflicting assumptions that one may encounter in male-female communications. Some of these apply only to sexually intimate relationships; most will apply to any heterosexual friend-ship. (Most same-sex intimate relationships are marked by some of these gender-role difficulties as well, because most of the difficulties are cultural rather than biological in or-igin. And, of course, some men and women behave "against type," taking on characteristics usually associated with the opposite gender.) Recognizing and respecting these typical obstacles is like having a map to the realm of communication between the genders—but remember, a map can't get you anywhere by itself. To negotiate the hazards successfully and reach the higher ground of un-derstanding requires the willingness to be changed by the journey.

Means vs. Ends

Most men operate from a rational and linear point of view that keeps an eye on objective facts and the bottom line, and places a high value on "fixing" things in a mechanistic or scientific manner. Women generally have a more in-tuitive and diffuse picture of reality that replaces objectivity with a strong sense of relationship, leading them to favor empathy, compromise, and consensus in problem solving. In the simplest terms, it might be said that women focus on means and men focus on ends in their dealings with the world around them.

Thus, men have traditionally excelled at fixing machines and women have done better at soothing the hurt feelings of their spouses or children. But Mr. Fix-it runs into trou-ble when he tries to find or enforce a purely logical solution for his wife's upset, and her ability to empathize can't repair an automobile. These functional differences are by no means biologically gender-bound, but they have been cul-turally reinforced for generations. Each kind of thinking has its time and place, of course—and both can be learned and taught. Women and men can help each other become well-rounded individuals who have both kinds of thinking at their disposal.

Vulnerability vs. Toughness

In most societies of the world, women are generally more comfortable than men in admitting and expressing feelings of hurt, warmth, and tenderness. Men seem to have a need to act as if they are not sensitive or vulnerable, with a consequent tendency toward expressing anger more freely than women. Part of this difference in expression stems from historically different roles in the family, as men have been expected to act as protectors and providers while women were expected to be caretakers and homemakers.

As feminism has brought more and more women into realms of commerce and politics formerly restricted to men, we have seen these sex-typed clichés of toughness and vulnerability subjected to much stress and strain. Some women have become unnaturally tough in order to "make it in a man's world," while many men feel threatened and angry that their traditional roles are apparently under siege. This is no doubt part of the motivation behind the "men's movement," which also seeks to help men uncover and redefine their emotional lives. This work is important as far as it goes, but I hope that we soon see an "understanding movement" to bridge the gap between men's and women's issues.

In my view, a crucial part of understanding men's toughness is to realize that it is their cover for a sensitivity which is at least equal to that of women. In that sense, toughness and vulnerability are really expressions of the same quality. For a man, the more vulnerable one feels, the tougher one must act in order to survive. For most women, reliance on mutual support is preferable to developing a tough exterior. Since men don't have the verbal capacity that women have for expressing their feelings of vulnerability, what men come up with as a substitute is either anger or emotional remoteness.

That is not to say that men will always appreciate being reminded of their true sensitivity, but it can be very helpful to women to remember that it is always there. Behind the anger is hurt and fear. The man who appears to be *un*feeling is far more likely to be without words for his feelings, and so unfamiliar with discussing them that he assumes it wouldn't be worth the trouble. His passionate reactions to the football game on television, however, should belie any notion that he has no feelings!

Power vs. Support

For years, men in the world of business have made deals both licit and illicit through their networks of power and play, extending from the golf course to the corporate boardroom. Traditionally, a sure result of men's power relationships has been to cut someone into or out of a deal or agreement, with money, prestige, and clout always figuring into the reward and punishment system. By contrast, women's communication networks have been characterized chiefly by mutual support and sympathy, although a punishing use of gossip can sometimes develop.

While conventional business patriarchies have by no means dissolved, I think it can be safely said that the hard boundaries between men's and women's networks are gradually disintegrating. But the assumptions of power versus support figure into home-front communications as well, when men come home from work and attempt to apply their workaday strategies to issues of intimate relationship and the family. As with all the dichotomies being explored here, neither one of these approaches to life is negative in itself, but either one can be damaging or insufficient without the balance of the other. Wielding power without offering support results in cruelty, resentment, and shortsighted solutions. But support without power can lead to indecisiveness and stagnant, codependent relationships.

Again, this is a typical arena of conflict between men and women that can become a learning exchange, if a medium of understanding like EP is deliberately applied by at least one partner in a discussion.

Closeness vs. Peace and Quiet

Comic Elayne Boosler has observed that most men want to be "really, really close to a woman who will leave them alone." This is an apt characterization of a frequent conflict in male-female relationships that have matured beyond the early romantic stage. Particularly after a couple has been living together for a while, the woman will want frequent check-ins and discussions about the health and quality of the relationship, whereas the man is content to assume that everything is okay and doesn't need talking about. The question of talking or not talking about things thus often becomes a power struggle that can add to whatever difficulties the couple may already be facing.

These opposing drives for closeness or peace and quiet again derive largely from each gender's typical insecurities in relating to parents, particularly the parent of the opposite sex. In our culture, little girls seldom receive sufficient tenderness or affirmation from their father, especially during the trials of adolescence. Thus they grow up with the habit of asking for something from men that they never received enough of when young. For little boys who depend on their mother for their sense of belonging in the world, the notion that Mother's love might not be solid or total is too frightening to question. (While little girls experience this fear, it is ameliorated by their same-sex identification with their mother, and later by cultural influences that encourage women's acceptance of support from both women and men.)

But for little boys, it feels safest simply not to question or examine the quality of the relationship with Mother. This establishes a habit of relating to females that leads the adult male to feel very threatened when his woman suggests that "we need to talk" or "we need to work on our relationship." If she's showing any emotion at this time— and she probably is—the subconscious effect on the man can be terrifying. Considering also his awkwardness about discussing feelings, he would much rather go out to play tennis, fool around with his power tools, or take a nap than talk about anything.

In general, I think this arena of conflict requires more courage on the part of men, to overcome their habitual anxiety about examining relationships and do their best to respond to women's entreaties. A rule of thumb I give to couples is that anyone who feels that their sense of closeness is threatened deserves a fair hearing as soon as possible. That doesn't mean the other partner must automatically agree that there's a serious problem or feel guilty about it—only that he or she must lend an ear to the other's feelings as soon as possible.

A significant reward for men in changing their habit of remoteness is that as they learn to respond to women's concerns more quickly, there will in fact be fewer disturbances of the peace. Another is the increase in romantic interest and responsiveness by women when their male partners become closer friends with them. Yet another is the nurturing support that women tend to offer their best friends.

Whenever a woman is perceived by a man to be nagging, it probably means that she has not received a fair hearing of her concerns in quite a long time. Working on closeness may indeed appear to threaten peace and quiet in the short term, but in the long term it's the only guarantee of stability and enthusiastic partnership.

The Familiarity of Loneliness

The four typical arenas of conflict we have just examined obviously do not cover all the typical gender differences one may encounter in intimate communications; I have not even touched on attitudes and perceptions revolving around sexuality itself. But I am less interested right now in cataloging differences than in proposing a means of ethical, respectful communication that has the potential to cut through them all. To do so, such a means of communication must approach the healing of the *fundamental* barrier to human intimacy: that we all live in unique and private worlds of personal experience. To become obsessed by gender differences is to focus on a secondary problem. Such a focus can easily lead to the unfortunate assumption that since we cannot erase sexual differences, we can never achieve a useful understanding of members of the opposite sex.

Besides, the emotional dynamic that drives most problems of intimacy has nothing to do with gender differences. The irony of selecting and relating to our primary intimate partners is that we are familiarity addicts: *We are accustomed to the way things have always been, even if that means a lot of unhappiness and isolation.* Thus we find it difficult to recognize or accept the very kinds of love and attention that we hungered for early in life. We are quite *unaccustomed* to getting what we need. That's why we will tend to be attracted to, and feel most at home with, the kind of person who makes us feel the same way we felt during childhood—no matter how unhappy we may have been as children. This person also provides us with another chance to try to win the kind of love we weren't able to elicit from our parents when we were young.

For instance, a woman who adored her strong, silent father—and grew used to being kept at arm's length from him—will tend to fall in love with an emotionally remote male when she grows up. A man who resented his mother, yet was used to her acting out the hidden emotional life of the entire family, will be drawn to a woman who proves to be much more dramatic and expressive than himself. (This particular kind of partnership is a shorthand summation of the typical emotional dynamic of the American nuclear family since the 1940s, by the way.)

In the long run, the person with whom we choose to repeat such familial roles and expectations will prove to be dissatisfying in the very ways that we've always been dissatisfied—and our greatest needs will continue to go unanswered as they always have been. This is the foundation for codependent relationships, in which intimate partners inadvertently support and prolong each other's neediness and inadequacy, rather than helping each other heal the wounds of childhood and discover true, adult intimacy. We are healed not by finding a perfect lover to fill in all our gaps for us, but by achieving *self-acceptance.*

And self-acceptance grows gradually from learning to feel compassion for all the kinds of pain that are inevitable in the human condition.

Healing Each Other

While everyone wants to be loved, relatively few of us are actually comfortable with the experience over the long run. What Ethical Persuasion brings to intimate relationships is a step-by-step process for achieving an understanding deep enough to lead to the mutual healing of self-doubt, woundedness, and alienation. As you learn to witness and care about each other's reality—no matter how bizarre or unreasonable some aspects of another's reality may appear—you offer each other a compassionate acceptance that will challenge the human status quo of loneliness and alienation.

The power of hearing and being heard in a mutual context of respect, understanding, caring, and fairness will not only overcome typical gender differences; it can eventually wear down the much more powerful resistance to believing in one's own beauty and right to exist on this earth. To become champions of each other's self-acceptance is to take up the rewarding work of healing each other. As real intimacy grows from this work, the struggle over differences is increasingly replaced by the playful enjoyment of each other's inherent uniqueness and gifts.

8

Bosses, Managers, and Employees

Will people who regularly practice Ethical Persuasion be able to prevent blowups from ever occurring in their sensitive communications? I doubt it. I've been using and refining the approach for years, and occasionally I still find myself in heated disputes that have to be patched up later.

Fortunately, it's been my experience that EP is a highly effective way of approaching such return engagements. It allows everyone to acknowledge and make use of the emotional intensity that led to the preceding blowup, instead of settling for contrite apologies or a glossing-over of feelings that may still be strong and pertinent. The result is that any seeming damage to the relationship can often be used to deepen it. That's why the veteran EP practitioner is able to regard almost any explosion in a delicate communication as a potential *accelerator* of understanding. And that can be a valuable foresight in circumstances where issues and feelings are just too hot to permit a positive resolution from the first go-around.

Communication blowups offer a distinct advantage to the EP practitioner because they yield dramatic displays of people's real feelings and intentions, even if they are stated only in negative or threatening terms. Everything is laid out on the table, as it were. From the EP point of view, that means the messages behind everyone's feelings are much closer at hand than they would be in a more restrained exchange. Thus the potential for achieving understanding, creative resolution, and greater closeness is enhanced.

In Chapter 1, the workplace dialogue between the young black female assistant manager of a computer store (Lenora), and her middle-aged white male superior (Martin), ended in an explosive exchange of threats. Rather than show how that conversation might have gone better in the first place, let's assume that there was no way to avoid the showdown between Martin and Lenora.

Instead, imagine that Lenora tells the whole story to an older woman friend, Anna, who has experience using Ethical Persuasion in corporate politics. She first advises Lenora that she must decide if this is the right time to take a confrontational stance against her company and try to force reversal of a decision already in place, with the likely consequence that she will soon become a full-time litigant and political activist rather than a store manager. Or does Lenora want to increase her likelihood of being promoted soon within the company, and increase her personal power and influence at the same time?

Lenora opts for the latter, but tells Anna that she doesn't simply want to back down and gain no concessions from

Martin or the company. She rightly feels that merely apologizing could set her up for being passed over and mistreated again, and her mentor agrees. Anna offers to coach Lenora in Ethical Persuasion, and they do some role-playing to prepare her for another encounter with Martin. Anna also helps Lenora write the following letter:

Dear Mr. Swanson,

I've been thinking about what happened between us in our meeting last Friday, and I'm still unhappy about not receiving a promotion that I feel I have earned. But to be perfectly honest, I'm not proud of how I handled myself in your office. I'd like to meet again and continue our discussion in a more positive manner. I'd like to hear your ideas on my future with the company, and discuss some kind of specific commitment for my advancement in the near future.

If you're willing to talk again on these terms, I'd much rather go that route than pursue the extremity of legal action to address my grievances. I regret that our last conversation was broken off in anger, but at least now we each have a better understanding of where we both stand. Perhaps we can make use of that knowledge to benefit both of us, as well as the company, in the long run.

Respectfully,
Lenora Diamond

From her experience with corporate authority, Anna warns Lenora to be prepared for a friendly but patronizing reception of this letter. "He's probably going to look at it as a little white flag," Lenora's mentor tells her. "Whatever he says for openers, remember to confirm and repeat it back to him before you state your case. Make sure he knows that you're really hearing him, because it will increase your leverage when it's time to ask for what you need from him."

By the time Martin's secretary calls Lenora with an appointment time, Anna has given her student an excellent introduction to Ethical Persuasion. Lenora approaches the meeting with the new, long-term goal of maximizing her personal power, rather than merely attempting to avenge a professional insult.

When Politics Get Personal: Building Personal Power

LENORA: Mr. Swanson, you've read my letter and had a chance to think about it, just as I have. I'd appreciate hearing your thoughts and feelings about the situation.

MARTIN: Lenora, first I'd like to get back to a first-name basis, okay? Beyond that, let me say I'm prepared to let bygones be bygones. Before this last position became available, I saw you as one of our outstanding managerial candidates, and I still feel that way. I can personally guarantee that you have a real future with this company; before too long, you'll be a manager for sure. I'm very glad that you've decided that's still what you want to pursue. So I don't think we have a problem here.

LENORA: That's good to hear, Martin—I appreciate that you don't feel hurt or resentful because of what happened between us in our our last talk. But let me make sure that I understand exactly what you're saying. It sounds like I haven't lost any points with you personally, and you'll be keeping my interests and desires in mind when the next promotion opportunity comes around.

In other words, I have just as good a chance at promotion as I ever did. Is that what you're saying?

MARTIN: Exactly. Absolutely.

[*Lenora has already pursued and completed Phase 1 of EP with Martin on the first point of their negotiation—where they stand at the moment—but she's aware that she has lost ground tactically and must remind him of her terms for this meeting. Thus she initiates Phase 2.*]

LENORA: Well, Martin, I have to admit that I still have some problems with this situation. I appreciate that you're not consciously bearing any grudge against me, because that would make our relationship impossible. But I'd like to remind you that I wanted this meeting in order to discuss a specific commitment of some kind about my promotion. I used that language in my letter for a reason; I mean you no disrespect, but I'm afraid I really need more than your personal reassurance that everything will work out.

MARTIN: [*Looking at his letter from Lenora*] Oh, yes . . . I see what you're referring to. Well, I guess we can talk this over in the months to come. I'm sure we'll work out something.

LENORA: Are you saying that you can't make a commitment to me in this meeting? In my letter I tried to be clear that I expected us to agree to something specific today; those were my grounds for coming to this meeting. I made that request because I remembered you saying in our last meeting that you had not handled Doug's promotion well and you "owed me one." Have I misinterpreted what you said?

[*Note that while Lenora reveals her negotiating position, she continues to check back with Martin on her understanding of his viewpoint. In most conversations, Phases 1 and 2 of EP will frequently overlap in this manner.*]

MARTIN: Let me think a moment. . . . Yes, I do remember saying that I blew it, and that I owed you one. You're right about that, but please understand that my mistake was not my decision to promote Doug—it was letting the cat out of the bag before I had talked to you. You have my promise that nothing of the sort will ever happen again, Lenora.

LENORA: I appreciate that, Martin, and I have enough respect for you and your experience to know that you're unlikely ever to make that kind of mistake with me or anyone else. I know you'll do that out of sheer professionalism. But if I understand you correctly, you're asking me to settle for that right now—your reassurance that you won't make the same mistake twice, and that we can talk about my promotion chances in the months to come. That's the end of it as far as you're concerned. Is that how you see it?

MARTIN: [*Hesitantly*] Well, yes. . . .

LENORA: All right. Let me try to explain why that doesn't strike me as the kind of commitment I need right now. Can you put yourself in my position for a moment, and see why I feel insecure about my future in the company? I've been passed over once, and if we're both honest I think we have to admit that my being black and female had something to do with it—

MARTIN: Look, now, I'm not biased against blacks *or* women.

LENORA: I don't mean to imply that you are, Martin. But can you honestly say that you aren't nervous about making a woman, let alone a black woman, a store manager? In your whole career, how many black women have you made managers?

MARTIN: There haven't been any, to tell the truth.

LENORA: So you don't have much ground for confidence in us, do you? You almost *have* to be nervous about it. When I was thinking this over, I tried to put myself in your shoes, and I could see what you would be risking to promote me. You're the person in charge of staffing at the manager level and your reputation is on the line with every appointment you make. Now, the clientele of all our stores is mostly white and male. Even if you personally don't have any race or gender prejudice, you can't say the same for customers, and other employees I'd be supervising, and the rest of the world! Some of this must have been going on in your head. Am I right?

MARTIN: Well, I wouldn't have come out and said it myself, but that's very perceptive on your part, Lenora. I do have to weigh all the unfortunate realities of the business against your personal attributes and experience. And that's probably what gave Doug the edge last time. I'm sorry that's how things are, but there it is.

LENORA: It's not news to me, Martin—I can take it. But can you understand why I feel insecure about my future in this company right now? After what's happened, can you understand why I might want something more concrete than I have in my hand at this moment? I really need to know that I'm not wasting my time in this company. I'm not asking you to agree with me, but can you understand where I'm coming from?

[*Now Lenora is approaching the end of Phase 2 of EP by asking for confirmation (not approval) of her viewpoint from Martin.*]

MARTIN: I think so, Lenora—I'm just not sure what I can do for you. What kind of commitment are you looking for?

[*Lenora proceeds into Phase 3, offering the first possible resolution for this negotiation.*]

LENORA: I want a written guarantee that I will be offered the next promotion to come up statewide. If I can't take it for any reason, I'll also have the first crack at the next one. Do you have a problem with that?

MARTIN: I'm afraid I do. The problem is that it's against company policy. If it were just up to me, I'd be happy to give you that guarantee. But this would involve talking to my superiors at headquarters and the regional manager. It would be very complicated.

LENORA: Can you blame me for asking for it?

MARTIN: No, I guess not. I'm just not in a position to guarantee it.

LENORA: Well, Martin, if you think it's a fair request, I'd like to know if you're willing to go upstairs and discuss getting such a guarantee for me. I'd like you to tell them that I need this kind of concession from the company for me to feel good about staying on. If you can do that much for me, I'll feel like the one you owed me has really been paid off.

MARTIN: Hmm . . . I'll need some time to think about it, Lenora. It's not that I'm unwilling to go out on a limb for you, but I'll have to figure out how to approach it. It could be mighty difficult.

LENORA: Do you mean it will be awkward for you to admit there was a problem with Doug's promotion and you have an uppity assistant manager on your hands as a result? Am I putting you in an embarrassing situation?

[*Note that Lenora is returning to Phase 1 of EP to bolster Martin's support of the resolution to this negotiation, cementing their alliance and augmenting her personal power in the process.*]

MARTIN: [*Chuckling*] Yes, Lenora, you are, but beyond that it's just a very unusual request. I'll be leaning hard on my reputation, that's for sure.

LENORA: I appreciate that, Martin, and I get no satisfaction from putting you on the spot. But perhaps you could point out to the guys upstairs that they have an affirmative action policy on the wall and very few minority managers out in the field. Perhaps you could turn this situation into an opportunity for everybody.

MARTIN: [*Laughing*] Maybe so, Lenora. At least I can honestly tell them that we've got a hell of a negotiator on our hands! I'm certainly impressed with how you've handled yourself here today, so I have more confidence than ever about your managerial potential. Right now, I can't promise you this will work out, but I will give it a try. I'll try to get back to you in a month. In the meantime, how about a raise to, say, eighty-five percent of a manager's pay? Will that help you hang in there awhile?

LENORA: I guess I'd be stupid to turn that down, Martin, but what's more important to me is some demonstration of faith in me by the company. More money right now is not my goal. I understand that you're making this offer because it's something you can approve right away, but I'm not asking for it. So do we both understand what I'm looking for?

[*Here Lenora is asking for a final Phase 2 confirmation of her value-driven position.*]

MARTIN: Absolutely. Let's leave the raise on the table and talk again when I have some word from upstairs. I'll do my best for you.

LENORA: Thanks so much, Martin. I appreciate your hearing me out and going to bat for me, I really do. I'm glad we've managed to turn this thing around between us. Now it'll be a lot easier to concentrate at work, that's for sure.

A Demonstration of Strength

By any standard, Lenora has completed a superb negotiation in her return engagement with Martin through a consistent application of Ethical Persuasion. She has not only rehabilitated Martin's impression of her, but has actually improved it by displaying communication skills he had not seen from her before. While not openly challenging his positional authority, she has procured a personal guarantee that he will make a definite, extraordinary intervention on her behalf.

This is proof of a distinct improvement in their personal relationship, because Martin is not professionally compelled to offer Lenora any kind of concession. He does so because she has clearly communicated what she needs in order to stay on with the company and maintain her self-respect. She has also reminded him that fairness and his own self-respect demand that he make good on the "debt" he incurred when he mishandled the announcement of Doug's promotion.

Of course, Lenora's future with the company is by no means guaranteed. Martin may fail to procure the promise from headquarters that she needs, and then she will be faced with the decision of whether to stay with the company (and perhaps take the offered raise), find another opportunity elsewhere, or file a discrimination suit after all. If she ends up doing the latter, her position will be stronger than when she first threatened Martin with such action, since her letter to him documents her attempt to deal with the issue in a responsible manner.

All in all, Lenora has demonstrated her real strength in the most positive way possible in this second encounter with Martin. In their first dialogue, her strength was plainly visible, but of little use to her or anyone else. At that time, Martin's idea that she had a chip on her shoulder was dramatically confirmed. In this talk, he is impressed by her maturity, confidence, and understanding—qualities that are both revealed and enhanced by her skillful use of EP.

Admittedly, not everyone would do this well after their first introduction to the principles and techniques of Ethical Persuasion. (And another superior might well prove to be more stubborn, authoritarian, and uncompromising than Martin.) Repairing such a breakdown in communication might prove impossible, or it might take more time and proceed more haphazardly. But Lenora's performance is by no means beyond the realm of possibility for an EP novice.

Reading Between the Lines

Lenora does have a head start in her second meeting with Martin because her dedication to self-respect is strong, and thus she does not fall prey to the kind of patronizing that he pursues at first: "I'm prepared to let bygones be bygones. . . . I don't think we have a problem here." Lenora sees immediately that Martin is assuming she has simply returned to the fold after contemplating the loss of her job; thus he can afford to ignore her request for a specific commitment about a promotion. Carefully, she pins him down on this attitude by restating it for him: "In other words, I have just as good a chance at promotion as I ever did. Is that what you're saying?"

Lenora is laying a trap here—an ethical trap, but a trap nonetheless. When Martin confirms that this is indeed the way he's looking at the situation, Lenora is in an excellent position to remind him that she's actually entitled to a *better* chance than she's had previously: "I remembered you saying in our last meeting that you had not handled Doug's promotion well and you 'owed me one.' Did I misinterpret what you said?"

When Martin admits that he does owe Lenora something but doesn't want to go beyond a promise that she will not be mistreated again, Lenora has achieved the kind of leverage she needs to make her case for a more specific commitment. She's eventually going to appeal to Martin's sense of fairness in order to take both of them beyond the status quo of corporate politics. But first Lenora must explore the background of Martin's anxiety about promoting her in the first place. She has a pretty good idea about some of the feelings he hasn't shared with her, so she must take a special approach to restating his position.

Empathic Guessing

When you are trying to confirm your understanding of someone who isn't revealing much of their thoughts and feelings, you may have to go beyond what they have actually spoken and make some empathic guesses about what's going on inside them. Lenora alerts Martin to this process by saying "I tried to put myself in your shoes" and then listing the thoughts and feelings that she imagined while trying to look at the situation his way.

Lenora also wisely acknowledges Martin's position of higher authority and responsibility: "You're the person in charge . . ." As a general rule it's smart to acknowledge a superior's authority and responsibility early, explicitly, and *respectfully;* muttering "You're the boss" with a disdainful sneer will only damage your bargaining position. A respectful acknowledgment, however, accomplishes two things: it establishes that you recognize the differences in function, responsibility, and relative influence between you and your superior, and it lets him or her know that you are able to deal confidently from your position nonetheless. (By contrast, superiors should generally assert their positional power in negotiations only as a last resort—and then apologize for having to do so, in recognition that personal power is always a better form of influence.)

At the conclusion of her summary of what "must have been going on in your head," Lenora asks Martin, "Am I right?"—which enables him to confirm, deny, or clarify her grasp of the pressures he has felt, but not confessed, in the relationship. Lenora could have taken a more confrontational stance, of course, by saying something like, "Admit it, Martin, you're just afraid of promoting a black woman!" This might have made her feel momentarily righteous—after all, the assertion is correct—but such a contentious manner of speaking probably would have been disastrous for the relationship as a whole. It would have put Martin on the defensive and wrecked the leverage Lenora had built so far.

It's much more effective for Lenora to concede that *if she were Martin, she would be afraid, too*—thus establishing a common ground and connecting their private worlds of experience. (Note that this is different from Lenora merely imagining herself in Martin's position, or his "shoes," in which case she might imagine herself being more courageous than he was. Imagining that you *are* another person, experiencing the faults and anxieties that person displays to the world, is far more empathic and influential.) Lenora is also letting Martin know that she recognizes we are all flawed human beings who are vulnerable to powerful societal pressures. It is the rare person among us who is consistently willing to bear those pressures alone in order to "do the right thing."

By offering Martin a *feeling alliance*—the sense that they are working together against enormous pressures that are not of their making as individuals—Lenora puts herself in the best possible position to enlist Martin in a *political alliance* to pursue her particular objective. He's taken aback by the request she makes, and at first tells her that it simply can't be fulfilled. By inquiring "Can you blame me for asking for it?" Lenora is essentially confirming the strength of the feeling alliance she has offered. When she receives that confirmation, she makes it clear to Martin that she simply wants him to make an unusual effort on her behalf—not to guarantee its success.

Converting Negativity to Growth

It's important to grasp what's happening beneath the surface here. Lenora is not merely offering Martin the chance to make good on his moral debt to her—she is actually converting the negativity of their first encounter into real growth in their relationship. Whatever the response of company headquarters to her request, Lenora can be assured that Martin understands and supports her concerns to a much greater extent than he has before. He affirms the progress in their relationship by complimenting her on her negotiating skills.

Then Martin throws Lenora a kind of curveball that's not unusual in corporate politics: he offers her a raise before he takes her request to his superiors. From a cynical point of view, it could appear that Martin is trying to buy off an upstart subordinate. If she takes the raise, he could feel that he's under less pressure to represent her aggressively. From a more sympathetic perspective, however, Martin might simply be trying to do what's within his immediate power to soften any disappointment that may be in store for Lenora.

Lenora could explore Martin's motives fully by initiating Phase 1 of EP again, but she decides to take a shorter route by reminding Martin that her request is *value-driven.* That is, she's less interested in material reward than she is in receiving reassurance that the company is willing to treat her with respect, understanding, caring, and fairness. And just in case Martin was hoping to get himself off the hook, Lenora is reminding him that she is not easily distracted from her long-term goals and fundamental values.

Changing the Nature of Power in the Workplace

In Chapter 3, I offered a new definition of power as "creative influence": the ability to add energy to any human interaction and create beneficial results exceeding normal expectations. This kind of power can be used and increased by anyone in any organization, regardless of their official position, because it *flows* from self-respect, personal competence, and dedication to fundamental values, and *grows* through the pursuit of ethical communication. Remembering that creative influence can always be wielded as one's own form of personal power is crucially important in professional environments where one may be hampered by lacking (or sometimes by possessing) positional power.

Using Ethical Persuasion in any kind of workplace conflict immediately brings one's personal power to bear on any of the faults or excesses of positional power that are creating problems between people. Note, however, that EP does not challenge any form of authority head-on; rather, it invites the complete and open exploration of all issues that are involved in a particular communication. These issues include how everyone experiences the problems at hand in their own private worlds, and how they *feel* about them—factors that are often left out in the business world's pursuit of the short-term bottom line.

In day-to-day organizational life, the problems of having or not having positional power do come up regularly. The sooner they are acknowledged and respectfully explored with EP, the sooner negotiations can be freed of threats, demands, posturing, and other artificial forms of communication.

Thus even the lowliest employee of the most rigidly

hierarchical corporation can have a democratizing effect on his or her organization by using EP whenever possible. Lenora provides an excellent example of this effect in her second encounter with Martin, as she gradually enlists a recently hostile superior in her campaign to gain fair treatment from her company. As a competent worker with a good reputation, she maximizes the leverage she's earned by using EP in the midst of conflict.

EP from the Top Down

Can a manager, company president, or CEO profit from the use of Ethical Persuasion in conflicts with subordinates? Let's imagine that Martin initiates the second dialogue with Lenora because he regrets his own behavior in their previous blowup, he wants to keep her in the company if at all possible, and he knows EP but felt "ambushed" by Lenora's emotional forcefulness in the first encounter. Wanting to rehabilitate the situation by using EP but not quite sure of what he can offer Lenora in specific terms, he invites her back to his office to talk things over.

Many people in positions of authority might feel it necessary to have a resolution in mind before such a conversation, but Martin trusts that reaching an understanding with Lenora will enable both of them to come up with a more creative solution than he can devise alone. He's willing to trade some of his positional power for personal power—especially since he's aware that he lost personal power in the first bitter and conflicted encounter with Lenora.

In this version, let's assume that Lenora does not arrive in a conciliatory mood. Still considering the pros and cons of filing a discrimination suit, she accepts Martin's invitation only as an opportunity to appear more diplomatic than she did in the first encounter. But she arrives with the intent to use whatever is said in this meeting to solidify her case against Martin and the company.

When Politics Get Personal: Regaining Personal Power

MARTIN: Lenora, I'm very grateful that you accepted my invitation to resume our conversation from last week. I'm sorry that it ended like it did, and I'm not proud of having threatened your position with the company. That's not the way I like to handle difficulties; I'd much rather settle things person to person, in a way that everyone can live with. But things just got out of hand and my feelings got the better of me. I wanted to invite you back here so we could start over, and to do that I need to make absolutely sure I understand where you're coming from. Would you mind telling me again how you felt about Doug's promotion, and the way I handled it? You can be absolutely honest with me, Lenora; I'm not here to defend myself.

[*Martin has initiated Phase 1.*]

LENORA: All right, Mr. Swanson. I think you passed me over for the promotion because you were afraid of promoting a black woman, and you let Doug know without telling me about it first because you don't have much respect or consideration for me. You and Doug are part of the old boys' network, and promoting him was the easiest thing to do. You knew I wouldn't like the news, and I'm definitely *not* one of the boys, so you figured you could let the bad news trickle down and I'd take it quietly like I'm supposed to. Sorry I didn't cooperate —maybe I just don't belong in this company.

MARTIN: Well, I hope I can persuade you to hang on a little longer, Lenora. It genuinely bothers me that you're still upset. I don't entirely agree with your view of things, but it's not hard for me to understand how you arrived at these feelings. Just let me make sure I've got it straight: To you, Lenora, the promotion and the way I handled it are all of a piece. Either way you look at it, I acted with prejudice against blacks *and* against women, and as far as you can tell, I represent the attitude of this company as a whole. To stay with us means you would always be playing against a stacked deck. Am I getting close?

LENORA: [*Uncertainly*] Yes, Mr. Swanson, that's how it seems to me.

MARTIN: Then I can see why you're still upset, and not at all enthusiastic about staying on here.

LENORA: No, sir, I'm not. I'm looking at all my options right now.

[*Phase 1 is completed; Martin can now state his viewpoint.*]

MARTIN: All right. Then I know where you're at. What I need you to understand is how much I *do* appreciate your skills and dedication. Even though you're younger and less experienced than Doug, I really did have you under serious consideration for the promotion, because I think you have tremendous potential. The company is lucky to have you, Lenora, and I mean that sincerely. Whatever prejudices I may have—and you've definitely given me reason to take a look at myself in that respect—the fact that you're black and female is also working *for* you right now. The fact is that it won't look good for me if I lose you now, especially if you make your complaints public. I wouldn't keep you on just for that reason, but I'm trying to level with you. I think it's in the company's interest *and* my self-interest to assure your long-term future with us. I'm just not sure of what I can offer you to rehabilitate the immediate situation. But I'm certainly open to practical, realistic suggestions for the short term.

[*At this point, Lenora could suggest the same solution she proffers in this chapter's first version of this dialogue—the guarantee that she receives the next available promotion—and this conversation could presumably proceed to a similar conclusion.*]

Ethical Persuasion and the Future of Organizations

By stating at the outset that he dislikes the use of his positional power ("That's not the way I like to handle difficulties") and is willing to surrender his defensiveness ("I'm not here to defend myself"), Martin initiates a significant change in the nature of his relationship with Lenora. He defuses their power struggle and acknowledges that her point of view is entirely justified from her position. Thus he is refraining from using his authority to assert that he must be "right" and she must be "wrong" (or that right and wrong are irrelevant because he's the boss). Instead, Martin is affirming that he and Lenora are two human beings with a problem to solve together. Fundamentally they are two people whose relative positions in their company mean only that they have different functions and responsibilities based on their experience and skills.

For Martin, the long-term advantage of establishing this kind of relationship is that he vastly improves his chances of being able to count on Lenora's loyalty and creative input in the future. (And even if she doesn't stay with the company, he is much less likely to be a target of her legal or personal hostility.) He's also learned that some of his personal prejudices may be getting in the way of his effective leadership and fair treatment of his employees, and he has the chance to work on those prejudices to improve his own performance and reputation.

For anyone in a leadership position in a modern organization, ethical communication offers the chance to change the nature of organizational life from a labor-versus-management struggle to the mutual and creative pursuit of *quality* in products, service, and the daily experience of work. Max De Pree, CEO of the Herman Miller furniture firm, made the point concisely in his book *Leadership Is an Art:* "When we talk about quality, we are talking about quality of product and service. But we are also talking about the quality of our relationships and the quality of our communications and the quality of our promises to each other. And so, it is reasonable to think about quality in terms of truth and integrity."

From my consulting experience, I'm well aware that many organizations are so steeped in authoritarianism, deceit, collusion, and disrespect that any talk about improving the quality of professional relationships may seem ludicrous to insiders at any level of power. When you cannot imagine an ethically bankrupt organization changing as a whole, it may seem pointless or even dangerous to pursue small changes within its daily operations. After all, whistle-blowers and other ethical reformers seldom enjoy much job security.

The advantage of EP in this regard is that it is designed to improve relationships on a one-to-one basis, not to serve as a frontal assault on an organization's unethical internal policies or outside politics. A rank-and-file employee who feels trapped within a company with a hopelessly repressive mindset may not be in a safe position to confront the CEO and lobby for dramatic change from the top down. But she could certainly use EP to improve her relationships with mail clerks, secretaries, managers, supervisors—anyone who crosses her path in a normal working day. The gradual increase in personal power that will accrue from daily dedication to ethical communication may eventually evoke more real change within an organization than dramatic confrontations with the top brass ever would.

However slow to progress one's own organization may be, it's undeniable that an ever-increasing democratization of the workplace is evolving in this country and across the world. Ethical Persuasion is just one of many tools and perspectives (including empowerment, self-directed work teams, and participatory management) that can speed the leveling of power differences between management and labor. In the tumultuous business climate of the 1990s, the ethos of winning through intimidation is clearly bankrupt. And the era of winning through understanding has only just begun.

9

Parents and Children

From generation to generation, popular child-rearing styles seem to veer back and forth between variations of "permissiveness" and "authority" (or "discipline"). Permissiveness tends to place parents in a position of allowing or catering to their offspring's every desire, while the disciplinarian attitude generally sacrifices the human rights and native spirit of children to parents' desire to shape and control them.

For a while during the last decade, our society saw the rise of a child-rearing style that mixed both attitudes: Children were given everything their affluent parents thought they would need to "get ahead" in life, which included excessive material goods and a forced acceleration of their education. Thus, parents could still control and mold their children while congratulating themselves on their exceptional generosity and foresight.

Authority and permissiveness follow each other in a cycle because each philosophy creates characteristic problems that the other attempts to correct. Overdisciplined children often grow up angry with their parents, then overindulge their own offspring as a result. Children raised permissively tend to become wayward, selfish adolescents whose behavior raises a societal hue and cry that we should "stop spoiling our kids." And so it goes, with very little real progress being made toward the potential of human families as *sacred centers of spiritual development*.

By spiritual development, I mean the capacity to learn and change throughout one's life span in the direction of ever-increasing self-acceptance, integrity, creativity, and intimacy with others. These nonmaterial goals are the primary focus of an *ethical* approach to parenting, the approach supported by the use of EP in important family negotiations. Later in this chapter, I will further define the differences between authoritarian, permissive, and ethical philosophies of child raising.

For now, keep these ideas in mind as you read the rerouting of the third dialogue from Chapter 1, in which Gene and Peg, the parents of fifteen-year-old Lisa, learn that she has lied to them about a ski trip she wants to take with a boyfriend. In this revision, Lisa's father becomes aware of the intensity of his own feelings at a crucial turn in the three-way conversation and asks his wife to help him out on the use of EP.

A Declaration of Independence: Preserving the Family Alliance

LISA: Um, Mom, you know that ski trip I told you about?
PEG: Ski trip? What trip was that, honey?

LISA: You know, the one I told you about last week. The one to Silver Valley.

GENE: Silver Valley? That's in the mountains up by Greg's campus, isn't it?

LISA: Yeah, that's right. Remember I told you that Greg would be there, too? He's going to meet our, uh, group from school.

PEG: Oh, that'll be nice. When is this happening, honey?

LISA: This weekend, Mom. We'll be going up Friday afternoon.

PEG: [*Putting down her fork*] Friday afternoon? Lisa, that's two days from now! You don't have anything ready.

LISA: Yes I do, Mom. It's not a big deal; I'm just going for the weekend.

PEG: How many of your friends from school are going?

LISA: Oh, I don't know. . . . There'll be ten or twelve people staying in the lodge. Greg will be there, and maybe some friends of his.

GENE: Well, it sounds like fun. Do you have to ride all the way up there in a bus, or what?

LISA: Uh, no . . . I'm gonna ride up in a car.

PEG: [*Looking worriedly at Gene*] You mean you're all going up in cars? Who's going to be driving you, honey?

LISA: [*Shifting in her chair*] Well, just one of the older guys, I guess.

PEG: Wait a minute, honey. Isn't this trip being chaperoned by some teachers? Why aren't they driving?

LISA: Oh, Mom, don't worry about it. I'll be okay. I told you Greg would be there—

GENE: I don't think you answered your mother's question, Lisa. Where are your teachers going to be? What kind of trip is this exactly?

LISA: [*Whining*] Dad, you don't have to make a big *inves-*

tigation out of it! Look . . . it was actually James who invited me. We talk at school sometimes, you know, and when he found out that some of his friends know Greg, he thought it would be fun if—

GENE: This is the boy with the drugs?

LISA: No! I mean, that was only one time. He doesn't do that stuff anymore, Dad. He's really okay, Dad. He's nice and you'd both really like him if you gave him a chance!

GENE: Well, you can just forget about that, miss. You've been lying to us about this trip, and that blows any chances you *or* this James could have with me. We try to give you a pretty loose rein, Lisa, but I won't put up with being lied to.

[*To Peg*] I think we'd better ground this little girl for a while, don't you?

PEG: Well, Gene, let's not be too harsh. I think we all need to talk things over, but obviously this trip is out of the question.

LISA: [*Crying*] I am *not* a little girl, Daddy! Why don't you trust me? Have I ever been bad?

[*At this point, the dialogue diverges from its course in Chapter 1, as Gene catches himself getting angry and asks Peg to help initiate EP.*]

GENE: That's not the point, Lisa. Making up a story like this is bad enough for me. . . . [*Looks at Peg, then Lisa*] Okay, wait a minute. I'm getting pretty upset here, and I can see you are, too, Lisa. Maybe your mother is right—we need to talk this over a little more. Peg, can you help me out here? I need a minute to cool off.

PEG: Lisa, this is the first time I can remember that you've ever lied to us. Can you help us understand why you felt like you had to do that? What's going on with you, honey?

LISA: [*Angrily*] I couldn't tell you I was going on a trip with James because you wouldn't let me go! Ever since I told Daddy about him you told me to just stay away from him. And you haven't even met him! I tried to tell you the whole story about what happened to James, but you wouldn't listen. You don't trust me anymore, but I haven't *done* anything.

PEG: [*Glancing at Gene*] Well, we might have been a little rigid about James at first. Gene, do you remember what you were feeling when Lisa first told us about him?

[*Peg has briefly pursued Phase 1 of EP with Lisa, who brings up a past conflict in which Gene acted on his feelings without reaching an understanding of how his daughter felt. Thus, Peg pursues Phase 1 with Gene to bring the current conversation up-to-date on a feeling basis.*]

GENE: Yeah, I remember. I was scared to death at the thought of Lisa dating some older boy who's been in trouble with drugs.

[*To Lisa*] It's my responsibility as your father to protect you from getting into situations where you could really get hurt. I hope you can understand where *I'm* coming from, okay? When you tell me you're interested in a boy who's been in some drug trouble, I'm sure as hell not going to say, "Fine, go out and have a wonderful time"!

LISA: But Daddy, I'm not stupid! If I wanted to start hanging out with druggies, would I even tell you about them?

I told you the truth about James because I *know* he's okay! And look what good it did me.

[*This high-energy conversation could still degenerate into a battle at this point, so Peg wisely restates Gene's and Lisa's positions for each other to calm things down.*]

PEG: Okay honey, let's make sure we all understand each other. Gene, it sounds like you're saying that the very idea of Lisa having a boyfriend who's been in some trouble was scary for you because you care about her so much, and so you wanted to stop Lisa from seeing James to protect her. Is that right?

GENE: That's it.

PEG: [*To Lisa*] And you feel like you're old enough and responsible enough to choose your friends wisely and talk to us about them. But telling us the truth about James just backfired on you the first time, so you had to make up a story the next time around. Is that how you feel?

LISA: I guess so, Mom. But I wasn't trying to get away with anything, honest! I have to start making choices for myself someday, don't I?

PEG: Of course you do, dear. But I think we'll have to be consulted on some of those choices for a while longer. Your dad and I know you're not just a little girl, but sometimes it's hard to know just how grown-up you are. Maybe you think your father was just being mean about James, but can you understand that he was really concerned about you?

[*Peg has just initiated a shorthand form of Phase 2 with Lisa on Gene's behalf.*]

LISA: [*Looking at Gene*] Yeah, I guess so. I know you love me, Dad, and I know it's wrong to lie. . . . But it's still not fair.

GENE: What isn't fair, Lisa?

LISA: It's still not fair to tell me that I can't see James when you don't really know anything about him.

PEG: Well, I think you're right about that, honey. I think we do need to get to know him so we can give him a fair chance. [*To Gene*] What do you say about that?

[*Now Peg is moving the discussion into Phase 3.*]

GENE: I suppose you're right. Lisa, I guess I have to apologize for prejudging your friend and making you feel like you had to get around us to see him. I just hope you really understand that I can easily get upset if I think you're in danger—and a few minutes ago, it was very upsetting to learn that you were lying to us. But I can see how I may have put you in a tough spot.

LISA: [*Mumbling*] It's okay, Daddy.

GENE: Good. But for right now, Lisa, I think your mother and I are both clear that you can't go on this trip, even if Greg is there to look out for you. Do you agree, Peg?

PEG: [*To Lisa*] I'm afraid so. I'm sorry, you'll have to tell James you can't go, honey.

LISA: [*Whining*] Mom!

GENE: I'm sorry we can't let you do what you want, but as long as you're living at home, we're going to have to call the shots sometimes. Do you understand what I mean?

LISA: Yeah, but it's still not fair. It's not *my* fault you don't trust James.

GENE: You're absolutely right, Lisa. But that's not the

point. We wouldn't let you go on this trip even if we thought James was the finest boy in the world. We may be wrong, but we think you're still just a little too young for that sort of thing.

PEG: We're not saying you'll never be able to go on a trip with a boyfriend, honey—it's just that we're not ready for it, even if you are. But I tell you what—why don't we have a barbecue in a couple weeks when Greg is home, and you can invite James over for the afternoon? Do you think he'd like that? Would you?

LISA: Oh, I don't know . . . everything feels messed up now. I'll talk to him at school tomorrow when I tell him the bad news.

PEG: [*Glancing at Gene*] Well, it's all right with us if you want to call him now, Lisa. Gene?

GENE: Sure. You can even tell him what bad guys we are, Lisa. Just no more secret plans, okay? I don't want you to feel like you have to lie to us anymore.

LISA: [*Sighing loudly as she leaves the room*] Oh, all right. At least I don't have to hide my friends anymore.

Reading Between the Lines

This dialogue illustrates some of the dynamics of Ethical Persuasion in a family situation in which there will often be more than two people involved and each person has a different perspective on the situation. One of the less obvious reasons that this conversation completely deteriorated in its Chapter 1 version was that Gene and Peg were not communicating well with each other about how the conflict with their daughter should be handled. The result was that the two people who were the most upset, Gene and Lisa, lost control of their emotions and the discussion turned into a power struggle between them, with alienating and potentially dangerous consequences. Peg was essentially denied her right to participate.

In this revision that assumes an understanding of EP by the parents, Gene recognizes the intensity of his feelings as a signal that he needs to back off for a moment. He is stunned by the revelation that Lisa has lied to him, and in a kneejerk reaction has resorted to his positional power to assert his control of her: "I think we'd better ground this little girl for a while . . ."

But when Peg disagrees ("let's not be too harsh") and Lisa starts to cry, Gene realizes that he's failing to be respectful, understanding, caring, and fair. His feelings are not "wrong," but what he has started to do with them is obviously not improving his connection with his wife and daughter. Were only he and Lisa talking, he might call for a time-out in order to check with Peg, or simply to allow himself to cool down before resuming the discussion. But since Peg is present and calmer than he, Gene is able to ask for her help—which certifies his respect for her as a parenting partner.

As Peg pursues an understanding between her husband and daughter, she skillfully states her own position in terms of her alliance with Gene: "Well, we might have been a little rigid about James at first." At this or any other point in the discussion, Peg and Gene could also have called a time-out to work out their own differing points of view. But Gene accepts his wife's shorthand negotiation here. She also gives him the opportunity to talk about his sense of responsibility and vulnerability as a father who loves his daughter very much, to which Lisa is able to respond more constructively than to his threatened use of positional power.

Still, Lisa is firm about the declaration of independence that this episode in her life represents for her. "I have to start making choices for myself someday, don't I?" she protests. Peg concedes the point, but reminds Lisa that the three of them are in a teaching and learning partnership on this and many other issues: "Sometimes it's hard to know just how grown-up you are." This admission of uncertainty paves the way for Lisa's understanding of her father's motives ("I know you love me, Dad") and her own error ("I know it's wrong to lie"), but Lisa proves to be a hard bargainer by pointing out, "It's still not fair to tell me that I can't see James when you don't really know anything about him."

Increasing Power with Apologies

At this point, Peg makes a crucial concession to Lisa ("I think you're right about that") and conducts another short-hand negotiation with Gene, asking him if it seems fair that they should meet Lisa's friend. By now Gene has cooled off sufficiently to apologize to his daughter for his earlier harshness—a sincere apology that vastly increases his personal power in the situation.

Many parents would fear that such an apology would actually weaken their hand and would instead resort to a defensive, authoritarian attitude: "It doesn't matter whether we're fair. We're your parents and we know better so you must listen to us regardless." Choosing authority with no regard to fairness may seem to be the most efficient short-term solution to many problems. But the likely long-term results of such a policy are later, more dangerous rebellions by children or, in some cases, the breaking of their spirit and their failure ever to learn real autonomy and self-respect. (The identical dynamic occurs in organizations whose empowerment programs founder because of the authoritarian style of old-guard middle and senior managers.)

It's important to note that Peg and Gene's concessions do not result in their capitulating to Lisa's wish to go on the ski trip, which they still think is unwise. They offer a further apology at having to assert their positional power in the situation, a kind of apology that I think is almost always appropriate when one resorts to authority, whether the scenario is the home or workplace. Peg goes so far as to admit that she and Gene retreat to their authority because of their own fear and insecurity ("It's just that we're not ready . . . even if you are"), not any inability of Lisa's to take care of herself. Revealing this vulnerability gives Peg and Gene the power to repair their feeling connection to their daughter, enough that she can accept their decision, however reluctantly. When they offer the resolution of meeting James in a reasonably comfortable family situation, Lisa begins to see that her parents respect and care for her as a maturing human being. In fact, getting that recognition was probably part of her motivation in provoking the situation in the first place.

It's also possible that Lisa feels secretly relieved that she does not have to fulfill her defiant plan. Adolescents sometimes overshoot their own confidence, especially when they are resentful of what they see as disrespectful interference in their lives by parents or other adult authorities. At such times, it's very important that young people feel the presence of their parents as older, trusted, and understanding *advisers,* not as controlling disciplinarians or laissez-faire, indulgent "pals." If parents focus on increasing, modeling, and teaching personal power to children, then they will find the use of positional power less necessary, and the growth of their children's autonomy less traumatic than the norm.

Respecting Children's Rights and Spirit

One of the most difficult challenges of parenting is striking a balance between *protecting* children and *respecting their rights*. For the most part, I believe our culture does not sufficiently respect the rights of children to determine their own destinies because it does not recognize the presence and power of their innate spirits—and their always-growing capacity for responsible self-management. Of course, if we as adults are not anchored to our own spiritual center by healthy self-respect and ethical intimacy with others, we will be slow to recognize the inner spirits of our children. Few adults in our culture have secure spiritual anchoring by the time they reach physical maturity. That's why parenting must be regarded as a new and profound learning phase in which children are seen as spiritual teachers deserving of parents' care *and* respectful attention.

Partly out of a natural concern for their survival and welfare as adults, we school our children to "fit in" to our economic system and cultural beliefs, drumming out of them some of their inborn creativity and originality. In any realm of education, the trick is to provide children with all the guidance and learning sources we can muster, without pushing them toward our "right answers."

This is important for two reasons. First, the answers that were or would have been right for us may not be right for our children. Second, it's sometimes crucially important for children to discover the right answers on their own—with our consultation or comfort always at the ready—whether or not those answers end up confirming our knowledge and experience. To do their own legwork, make their own mistakes, and locate their own sources of wisdom is indeed one of the most precious developmental rights of children. If parents *embody and model* the fundamental values of respect, understanding, caring, and fairness, children will inherit a healthy foundation for exploring the world on their own.

"Staring Through Your Forehead at the Wall"

I learned an important lesson about children's rights in relating to my son Carl, from whom I learned more about parenting and the human spirit than from any book I've ever read. When he was about eleven, the two of us were hardly speaking, as our stubborn streaks were rubbing up against each other in the worst possible way. As an award-winning psychiatrist, I thought I had most of the answers to the challenges of human development, and I was far too eager to give them to Carl in order to accelerate his own growth. I just couldn't figure out why he wouldn't listen to the learned wisdom of his loving father! Our numerous conflicts as he entered adolescence finally convinced me that we would either learn to cooperate or at least one of our spirits would be broken. Fortunately, with his mother's help, I learned to get out of his way over the years, and now that he is a young adult we have an unusually close and mutually supportive relationship.

Carl once summed up our early conflicts this way: "You know, Dad, whenever you called me on something, you were inevitably 'right' about what I should be doing, but it seemed like you were really asking me to confirm or deny that you were right, not just giving advice on a take-it-or-leave-it basis. I could usually see that you were right, but I felt as if I would somehow disappear if I gave in. So instead I would just sit, staring through your forehead at the wall behind you, trying to make *you* disappear. I hated you for being right, loved you for caring, and I knew that I would die before I'd tell you that you were right."

Carl's message was not that he had been stubborn just for the hell of it, but that at age eleven or twelve he was exploring and fighting for his autonomy as a human being. When you have your autonomy as an adult and parent, it can be difficult to remember just how vital that issue is to young people—unless you deliberately pursue an understanding of their feelings. Ethical Persuasion enables parents to avoid stepping on their children's rights to grow and learn at a natural pace, instead of just assuming that "Father (or Mother) knows best." Parents, like therapists and bosses, often pull rank not because they really know best, but because they lack faith in their "subordinates." And a lack of faith can always be traced to inadequate respect and understanding.

It's also important for parents not to assume that schools, churches, or other social institutions know what's best for their children. In Carl's later adolescence, he began to have what school administrators often call "problems with authority." On one occasion a busy high-school teacher asked him to get a film projector from across the campus but neglected to give him a hall pass for the short walk. When a vice principal stopped Carl and asked for his pass, Carl explained what he was doing and why he didn't have a pass. The vice principal then said, "Go back to your class and get a pass."

Carl replied, "Why?"

The administrator said sternly, "Because I said so!"

At this point, Carl shrugged his shoulders, walked out of the school to his car, and drove home. After he had weathered several such encounters with school authorities, Judy and I encouraged Carl to quit high school and enroll at a fine arts academy, where his interests would be better served and he would not have to put up with abuses of positional power. I know that many parents would say that a child should obey school authorities in all cases because of the overwhelming "discipline problem" in our schools. But I think we really have a "mutual respect and understanding problem" in our schools—a problem that admittedly begins most often at home and gets dumped on schoolteachers and administrators who are ill equipped to solve it.

Three Kinds of Child Rearing

Earlier in this chapter I defined the prevailing philosophies of child rearing as either permissive or authoritarian and suggested that EP can serve as the centerpiece of an ethical philosophy that better serves the inner spirit of children and the health of families. Following is a brief elaboration on the differences between these three approaches on a few key issues of parenting. This is adapted from material I developed with the assistance of my daughter, Natalie, a master's graduate of Harvard's School of Education.

Issue: A Child's Inherent Qualities

Authoritarian: Children are believed to be born with both good and bad (evil, or original sin) in them. The good must be encouraged and the bad must be controlled, disciplined, and punished.

Permissive: Children may be seen as inherently good, but their mistakes may never be pointed out or corrected because correction might hurt their feelings and could be misinterpreted as punishment. Permissive parents will go to great lengths to avoid causing hurt or exercising authority.

Ethical: Children are seen as inherently good. With encouragement, support, and guidance of their inner spirit, they will flourish and contribute positively to society. Like everyone, they make mistakes while they learn to be respectful, caring people, but efforts should be rewarded and mistakes pointed out, not punished.

Issue: Children's Status

Authoritarian: Children belong to parents, who have the right and responsibility to mold them according to the parents' model of propriety. Everything a child does, good or bad, reflects on the family. Thus, parents must try to control children's appearances and actions. Parents are in charge because they know best. They remain fully in charge until children reach an arbitrary age (eighteen, twenty-one) or until they can support themselves financially.

Permissive: Children may be given freedom to "work things out on their own" in lieu of cultivation and guidance; parents may thus abdicate their responsibility as advisers. Parents may also encourage children to be on their own before they are ready; thus they are likely to get the message that they are an unwanted burden.

Ethical: Each child is a precious, unique, and temporary gift on consignment to the family as a privilege and sacred trust. Parents must honor each child's right to be protected, cultivated, and appreciated, and to learn how to handle freedom and responsibility. Parents are initially in charge because infants are born helpless and must depend on their parents' capabilities for survival. Parents gradually yield authority and responsibility in response to evidence of the increasing competence of their children.

Issue: Love and Responsibility

Authoritarian: Love is merely the natural bond of parents and children and is unconnected to the development of responsibility. Responsibility is synonymous with obedience to authority and conformity to external standards of propriety.

Permissive: Parents' love may be given only in the form of unconditional affection, which is assumed to make up for any lack of understanding or a failure to model and inspire personal responsibility. Sometimes a naive belief in the child's spirituality substitutes for a healthy sense of parental responsibility.

Ethical: Parents recognize love (that is, respect, understanding, and caring about others' feelings and well-being) to be the source of self-acceptance and responsible, considerate behavior. They teach and model ethical communication and personal power to help children establish a strong contact with their spiritual center, knowing that real morality arises from deep understanding and acceptance of oneself and others.

Issue: Self-Respect and Success

Authoritarian: Results and appearances are the major priorities. Self-respect is considered either a by-product of success or not explicitly considered at all.

Permissive: Fulfillment and self-respect may be confused with pleasure-seeking and self-indulgence, or success and wealth.

Ethical: Earning self-respect through honest, strong efforts is the highest priority for all family members. Personal fulfillment is valued over mere success as defined by wealth, prestige, power, or winning. Parents' modeling of personal power enables children to develop a strong sense of inner worth and valuation independent of external failures or achievements.

Issue: Feelings and Their Expression

Authoritarian: Each family member has a responsibility either to maintain a polite decorum for the sake of not upsetting others, or to endure emotional outbursts without respectfully exploring their cause. Family members rarely admit to feeling hurt or vulnerable.

Permissive: Everyone (or certain family members) may be allowed to act out their feelings without pursuing healthy communication or mutual respect.

Ethical: Sharing and caring about individual feelings, including strongly painful or negative feelings, is understood to be necessary to the ongoing health of the family. No one is forced, but everyone is encouraged to explain respectfully their feelings with confidence that they will be explored and cared about.

Issue: Negotiations

Authoritarian: Parental authority in family decisions is absolute; parents neither respect nor solicit children's opinions and each parent often acts unilaterally. Secrets between family members are permissible for the avowed purpose of protecting someone from feeling hurt, or the whole family from becoming upset.

Permissive: Negotiating of any sort may be perceived as unnecessary hard work; everyone tends to go their own way as much as possible. Paradoxically, permissive parents may resort to harsh and inconsistent authoritarian measures when problems escalate to crisis proportions.

Ethical: The parental partnership is a sacred trust and the model for all family negotiations. Parents operating as equals accept ultimate responsibility for policy-making decisions, after children's opinions have been fully heard and seriously considered. Secret coalitions between family members (on any issue more serious than surprise birthday parties) are intolerable.

Issue: Freedom and Limits

Authoritarian: Limits are specifically set over a wide range of activities and behaviors, and tied to an explicit system of external reward and punishment. Children must behave well; otherwise they will be punished. If they transgress and are not caught, they can make a "clean getaway," since an inner sense of right is not the focus. (However, repeated violations of their inner sense of right will cause children to feel bad over the long term, whether or not they are caught and punished.)

Permissive: Limits may be set only reactively, and then punitively, when children's irresponsible behavior ultimately hurts someone or causes other serious damage.

Ethical: The number of absolute limits for children is kept as small as possible, allowing as much freedom as children demonstrate they can handle. Limits that are enforced all involve caring for the human spirit. They include honesty with one another, respect for self and others based on sensitivity to feelings and pursuit of one's inner sense of right, and prohibition against violating each other's privacy or physically hurting one another. It is assumed that each person behaves honorably because it feels right and good to do so. If one violates basic values, the consequences will be felt within, whether or not others are aware of the violation. Repeated violations do not entail a series of punishments. Instead, they call for more frequent and intensive attempts at ethical communication between parents and children, perhaps with professional assistance.

Too Much to Ask?

Considering all the problems that parents must face today in safeguarding, feeding, and educating their children, is the adoption of an ethical approach to child rearing simply too much to ask? On the contrary, I feel that it is the only thing we can ask of ourselves as parents that is sufficient to enable our children to reach their full potential in a dangerous world which no longer has clear and fixed societal standards.

Authoritarian and permissive approaches are "outside-in" philosophies relying on the imposition of parental standards of conduct or the abandonment of any parental responsibility to inculcate values of a healthy relationship. Ethical child rearing, by its emphasis on the integration of values and feelings within family politics, is an "inside-out" philosophy. It helps children develop their own internal guidance system for finding their way through all the shoals, hazards, and minefields they will face on the way to maturity.

Changing one's entire philosophy of upbringing overnight is nearly impossible, especially if one was raised by authoritarian or permissive standards that are "bred in the bone." But altering the direction that a troubled family is going can begin with a single step: committing to the use of Ethical Persuasion in all serious family negotiations, and following its steps as far as possible in each specific encounter.

When things break down or become too hot to handle —as they surely will in any family's initial forays into EP—then the commitment to change means picking up again as soon as possible where the process of pursuing understanding was broken off. Resuming the process is, of course, the parents' responsibility, although children who have begun to learn the ropes of EP may pick it up instinctively and sometimes lead the way. Mediators or counselors skilled in family communications may also be quite helpful in the rough spots.

But parents who are willing merely to *attempt* EP will already be increasing their personal power—and decreasing the need for control, regimentation, repression, and all the other exhausting methods of authoritarian child rearing. Permissive parents who are afraid of exerting control will discover that EP provides a means for understanding and encouraging their children's spirit without either controlling them or simply cutting them loose into a world for which they may not have been sufficiently prepared.

The most difficult part of Ethical Persuasion is the decision that must precede its use: the decision to change in the service of greater respect, understanding, caring, and fairness for oneself and others. Even a little willingness to change from the inside out can yield immense and unexpected rewards of understanding, intimacy, and problem solving.

Children change all the time right in front of our eyes;

it's their full-time job. What adults and parents need to remember is that we're still changing, too. As our bodies age, our inner spirit is either dying from inattention and fear-driven suppression or being continually refreshed by our courageous self-investigation, creative expression, and ethical communication with others. The choice that we make for our own spirit is the choice we are teaching to our children.

10

Difficult People and Extra-Difficult Situations

Changing one's habits is never easy. My career as a counselor, teacher, and author has been devoted to helping people change their familiar but self-destructive habits of thinking, behaving, and relating, and I've never been able to tell anyone, "Don't worry. The change you want to make in yourself will be a snap!" Ethical Persuasion is a simple but challenging approach to changing one of the most intransigent habits of so-called human nature: defending oneself in emotionally charged communications. This habit makes us not only poor listeners, but poor explainers of ourselves as well.

How many times have you heard people shout threats or insults during an argument, only to follow them up with, "I'm sorry, I didn't mean that"? What's going on is that powerful but poorly understood feelings are surfacing in a person's awareness too rapidly to be accurately interpreted and carefully phrased. The feelings are authentic, and thus are really "meant" in their raw, nonverbal form. That's why the apologies that follow sometimes sound hollow. But as the feelings come into play in a situation that the person perceives as threatening, they are exaggerated into inaccurate, accusatory, and self-defensive language. Blaming and self-defense always preserve or intensify one's separateness from others.

Imagine, for instance, that a loud and bitter fight between a couple reaches a crescendo when one of the partners (male or female) shouts to the other, "I wish you were dead!" After a shocked silence, the person who shouted says quietly, "I'm sorry, you know I didn't mean that." The other person replies in a resentful, hurt-filled voice, "But I think you did. You really wish that I wasn't around at all." Then *that* painful misunderstanding becomes fodder for further argument.

What the first person felt, but could not say clearly, probably went something like this: "I hate that we're arguing like this when we say we love each other. I'm terribly confused because I care about you a lot and feel threatened by you at the same time. It shouldn't be this way between us. I wish I could change it, and make you stop saying these things, right now!" What the person actually says, out of bewilderment and fear, does actually force a pause in the argument—but not to any good effect.

It's no wonder that many people strive to suppress feelings in sensitive communications by "keeping things rational." It seems to them that human connections can best be preserved if no one gets upset, for everyone knows that strong feelings can easily overwhelm rational decision making, common sense, and respectful communication. But I think that almost everyone misidentifies the culprit here. Feelings are not the problem; the habit of misunderstanding and misusing them to defend oneself is. The crucial question is whether such a universal human habit can be changed.

The Painfulness of Self-Defense

By using EP over the years as a way to break my own habits of attack and self-defense and gradually replace them with the habit of pursuing mutual understanding, I've become more and more aware that *defending myself and attacking others always makes me feel awful.* My chest gets tight, and I feel cornered by whomever I'm talking to. Instead of listening carefully in order to achieve understanding— which would increase both my knowledge and personal power—I focus on "weak spots" in the other person's expressed viewpoint, ready to pounce upon them and prove my rightness or superiority whenever I can. In an attempt to preserve myself exactly as I am, I actually become smaller and less powerful. It's no coincidence that I feel more and more childish the harder and longer I defend myself.

Giving up self-defense and accepting one's vulnerability is a crucial part of self-acceptance; *for when we defend ourselves, we are really maintaining our self-doubt.* That's why we come across to others as being insecure at the very moment that we may believe we're looking invincible. Like children, we are still confusing bad feelings with being bad inside, and trying to deny the badness. But if we have no doubt of our inner worth, we can be open to negativity from other people—we can even be hurt by it—without feeling the need to lash back. The person who can turn the other cheek is not a martyr if she knows how to give her own inner spirit care and compassion for the wounds dealt her by the world.

People who become aware of the pain and anxiety they create while defending themselves are better equipped to deal with the discomfort that comes with the Ethical Persuasion process, particularly during Phase 1. The largely unfamiliar unease of giving up self-defense and laying oneself open to the hostile, strange, or simply unexpected feelings and opinions of others requires a kind of concentration that may be new for many people. A friend of mine who uses EP in his work as a business consultant describes this concentration as an "altered state" wherein he becomes aware of his desire to defend himself, but silently turns it around to tell himself: "Okay, I'm going all the way through this unpleasantness to the very end. I'm going to hear this person out fully and completely, and demonstrate that I absolutely grasp his point of view. I will not attack, I will not defend, and I will amaze everyone with my will to understand."

This radically constructive attitude shows that the phase of exploring the other person's viewpoint in EP need not be perceived as a period of passive listening. In fact, the work of achieving understanding is much too hard ever to be considered passive. If someone really is attempting to attack or offend you, it may be impossible to accept their words in a soft or loving state of mind. But you can turn such a difficult circumstance into an opportunity for increasing your personal power by shifting the energy of self-defense toward what might be called *fierce understanding*. The chances of disarming a genuine opponent this way—with careful listening and painstaking restatements of his or her viewpoint—are much greater than if you simply attempt to out-argue this person. The only reason this is not widely known is that it is not widely attempted! In most cases, however, what one will discover by learning to give up self-defense is that *self-defense creates more of our misery than what others actually say or do to us.* It is not uncommon for highly defensive people to expect the worst from others and then be unable to hear anything else. Indeed, they may ignore or misinterpret messages of caring and compassion in order to hold on to the idea that they are unloved and constantly under attack. Even the person with average defenses can be slow to hear and understand another's point of view because the internal argument with one's own fears takes up most of the available energy and attention, drowning out the other person's intent and message.

The Familiarity Principle Revisited

Self-defensive styles of communication demonstrate the "familiarity principle" I have referred to earlier in this book: *You cannot act or be treated in ways that are different than those you are used to—even if those ways are better—without becoming increasingly uncomfortable.* However, the awkwardness and anxiety that go along with acting or being treated better than you are used to is *the discomfort of growth* which, with a little experience, can easily be distinguished from the tension one feels in self-defensive struggles to preserve the status quo of one's personality or experience.

For one thing, the discomfort of growth is most likely to be triggered by a deliberate act that serves the values of respect, understanding, caring, and fairness in regard to yourself and others—whether that act is initiating Ethical Persuasion in an important conversation or simply accepting praise when you're more familiar with negative criticism. By contrast, self-defensive reactions are more likely to be thoughtless and impulsive and to serve only the value of self-preservation. Self-preservation may be an appropriate value when confronted by a mugger on a dark street. It doesn't work so well in the context of intimate, familial, or professional relationships, where better understanding and greater intimacy are primary goals.

Another way to distinguish the discomfort of growth from the anxiety of self-defense is by what follows each experience. With few exceptions, the exercise of self-defense in difficult communications will make one more isolated, lonely, and negatively disposed toward healthier relationships. Also, the learning potential of self-defensive patterns of relating is very low. One is more likely to seek only corroboration for long-held points of view than to accept new information or try out novel perspectives on any subject under discussion.

By contrast, the growing pains of personal change result in one becoming more open-minded, better connected to other people, more self-respecting, and stronger and more peaceful overall. The habit of self-defense presumes that one's personal power is under attack and must be preserved at all costs. But it is only the dedication to growth and self-change that actually *increases* one's personal power and decreases the potential for conflict in important relationships.

The truth is that most of us are actually less afraid of being attacked by others than we are of *becoming all that we could be*—simply because our potential as excellent communicators and more caring, wiser human beings lies in the realm of the unfamiliar. That way leads to our spiritual reality, wherein we are not nearly so separate as we experience ourselves daily. It is really the end of separation that we fear, because we cannot imagine what it would feel like not to be fundamentally alone and always clinging to the mirage of control. Again and again you are likely to find that the greatest difficulty in pursuing Ethical Persuasion is the challenge of following your own path of positive change into the unknown territory of deep understanding, cooperative partnerships, intimacy, and joy.

When Others Refuse to Understand

Still, you may find yourself in situations in which your commitment to mutual understanding and personal change is firm, but you encounter overt resistance from someone who has no interest in hearing your view. Suppose, for instance, that you have heard someone out thoroughly, confirmed with him your understanding of his point of view, and are ready to initiate Phase 2 of EP. "Now I'd like to explain my point of view," you say, to which the other person replies, "Well, I have no interest in hearing it. I've said what I wanted to say, and frankly I don't care what you think."

Is the conversation over? If the other person leaves at that point, the answer is obviously yes, and you will have to make a determination as to whether this particular relationship warrants a return engagement. (More about this shortly.) In most cases, however, you would probably have the opportunity to pursue some understanding of the other person's refusal to hear you out, in the same Phase 1 manner that you would pursue an understanding of any new piece of information. You might say something like:

"Let me make sure I understand you. We both agree that I've heard you out thoroughly and that I have a good handle on what

you think and feel about the matter at hand. But now you're saying that you have no interest whatsoever in giving me the same kind of fair hearing, so that we might reach a mutual understanding/find a creative solution to our problem. Is that right? I need to be certain that you absolutely don't want to hear me out, so that I'm sure where we both stand on this matter. Without your help, I'll have to decide where I should go from here on my own."

Depending on your gut feeling about the circumstances and the other person's resistance, you may want to offer some help on clarifying his stance:

"Let me make sure I've got this straight. Despite the fact that I've taken the time to understand your viewpoint—and despite the fact that you've agreed I really do understand—now you're saying that you don't want to listen to me. Is that just how you feel at the moment, and you need a break to think things over? Or are you saying that you'll never be interested in giving me a fair hearing? I'll be happy to take a time-out for your sake, but if it's not going to make any difference, then I need to know where I stand."

The last option is important to consider because EP's appeal to fairness may trigger a delayed reaction in some people. Oddly enough, someone who is accustomed to being poorly understood may actually become suspicious about all the attention given to his point of view during Phase 1. If he feels that being understood has actually undermined his self-righteous position, he may resort to a self-defensive reaction of defiantly withholding his own understanding.

But I believe that fairness is one of the fundamental values of the human spirit, a value that hardly anyone can long ignore. If you have modeled fairness in your encounter with a resistant person, there's a good chance that your example will have delayed but positive effects on him in the long run, after he has had a chance to reflect on his unfair behavior and make a different choice. If you can keep the door open for later renewal of your discussion, you may find that an initially recalcitrant person will gradually soften up and allow you a fair hearing.

If it becomes plain at any point that you will not be given a chance to state your viewpoint, then you will have to make the determination of whether the relationship in question is worth saving. Assuming it is, then you'll have to reapproach ethical communication in the relationship at every opportunity and from as many angles as possible. You may want to enlist the help of friends, colleagues, or mediators along the way. If you *don't* want to be in the relationship but have little choice in the matter—perhaps you have a boss or parent with positional power over you who's not interested in listening—then you will have to look at the bigger picture of your life, of which this particular relationship is only a part.

The social support of other, healthier relationships can help you endure the one that is unhealthy. And as long as you are making your best effort to relate to a difficult person with respect, understanding, caring, and fairness, then you will be earning greater self-respect and confidence, and gradually increasing your personal power. Eventually the dysfunctional relationship will either end or change for the better. The more forgiving you can be of its chronic failings, the less likely you will be to resort to retaliatory measures, thus maintaining your self-respect by holding to the higher moral ground. Then it will be easier to move beyond the unhealthy relationship or help move it into a new, healthier phase.

When Others Reject Understanding

Let's turn the tables and imagine that you have initiated Phase 1 of EP with someone who makes it clear that she doesn't want to be understood. Withholding answers to your questions and refusing to confirm your grasp of her point of view, she demonstrates that she finds safety and familiarity in the mindset that no one understands her or really wants to. Her suspicious air suggests that she thinks the only reason someone would question her about her thoughts, feelings, and desires would be to gain an advantage on her. To this kind of resistance you might say:

"I feel very badly that we're not connecting here. You may not care, but I truly wish that I could understand you better. The more curious and concerned I am, the more tense it seems to make you. That's definitely not what I want to do! Something's going wrong, but I don't know what it is. Is there any way you can help me to understand? I'd certainly like to, and I want you to know that."

Perhaps the other person responds that she doesn't need your sympathy or understanding, for she can do just fine by herself. Then you will need to remind her that you value your relationship with her and you have an interest in its improvement:

"Look, you may see me as patronizing, but I have a reason for talking to you. We have a problem/We're in a committed relationship/We have to work together, and I care about you whether it matters to you or not. It also makes me feel lonely/treated unfairly/not respected to be kept at such a distance. I hope you're willing to risk opening up a little on the chance that my motives are sincere."

If the other person says anything at all in response to this, you can apply the steps of Phase 1 to repeat it back to her, then clarify and confirm your understanding—while expressing your appreciation of her willingness to open up to you. The relationship might then be well on its way to a healthier state before the other person becomes aware that her defenses are giving way. If her resistance to being understood remains firm, your options are similar to those in the previous example. You will have to decide on the importance of the relationship to you and whether it warrants further attempts at a breakthrough in understanding. Again, waiting a few days after each of these attempts would be advisable, to see if your ethical behavior has delayed effects.

"Tough Love"

A passionate and relentless emphasis on achieving understanding with even the most difficult and recalcitrant people is what I call "tough love." The more popular version of tough love implies the aggressive imposition of rules, restrictions, and disciplinarian environments on people (often young people) who have repeatedly run afoul of the law or the expectations of their families, schools, or communities. This kind of tough love is usually imposed in the name of caring and is generally seen as a corrective to a lack of discipline in the troublemakers' formative years and recent life-styles.

But I believe that most troubled children suffer from growing up in a family culture deficient in mutual understanding and respect. If the EP brand of tough love is used, focusing on correcting those spiritual deficits of children's upbringing—supplemented with disciplinarian measures only to keep troublemakers from hurting others or breaking laws while their spirits heal—then I think this firm but gentle approach can have profound and long-lasting effects. If harsh behavioral measures are enforced merely as punishment or are enforced as a show of so-called strength in the absence of emphatic attempts at understanding, then tough love is doomed to fail in the long run.

Most young people in trouble are *alienated from understanding and caring* on both the receiving and the giving ends. Parents who are trying to establish better communication with their alienated kids can find a useful clue by taking a look at how comfortable they are with the young, childish parts of themselves, the pain and playfulness of their own "inner children." Parents who disdain the internal reality of an extremely needy, vulnerable, and often wounded part of themselves are the most likely to have great difficulty finding a common ground of understanding with their offspring. Tough love, in the form of Ethical Persuasion pursued both tenderly and adamantly within the family circle (perhaps with professional assistance), may lead such parents to change their own attitudes and behavior more profoundly than their children. For even the most troubled children are closer to the sanity and vitality of their native spirit than parents who have been alienated much longer from their own source of innocence and creativity.

EP When Time Is Short

A difficulty with Ethical Persuasion in all kinds of circumstances is that it can sometimes require a lot of time for people to listen carefully to each other, restate each other's viewpoints, confirm their mutual understanding, and devise creative resolutions. It may also *sound* like it will take an enormous amount of time before it is even attempted.

Whether it actually takes up more time in the long run than arguments, chronic misunderstandings, and failed relationships is another matter. Even if it does, I feel that EP's capacity to heal human discord is worth any amount of time it requires.

However, there may be circumstances in which the time available for problem solving or the resolution of conflict is unavoidably short and it seems unlikely that the phases of EP can be pursued in full. Before presuming that it cannot be pursued at all, it's important to ask yourself (and anyone else involved, if possible) these questions:

- Is there any way to delay the solving of the particular problem at hand while we pursue a better understanding among ourselves? Is there really no time to "sleep on it" after we've reached a mutual understanding of the issues?
- Are we focused on finding an immediate solution *because* we do not want to deal with our conflicted opinions and feelings? And are we short of time because we have pursued short-term solutions over understanding in the past? If so, can we risk a delay in decision making while we take a more productive route this time?
- Can we establish a temporary solution for the problem at hand (e.g., separating instead of divorcing, taking a vote, relying on the judgment of someone with positional power, calling on an outside expert) while we initiate and pursue EP for the purpose of finding a long-term solution that is more satisfying for everyone?

Such questions are important to consider when time is short because the urgency of a situation is often defined as much by our *feelings* as by deadlines and other objective circumstances. Our hunger for immediate satisfaction can provoke us to foolish impulsiveness, or we may be fed up with unsolved problems or chronically dysfunctional relationships. Then we may decide that "the end is near" or "something must be done immediately" when, as a matter of fact, a better understanding among all the people involved could actually *create* additional time and patience for problem solving.

In family and organizational consulting, I've seen that parents and managers are particularly prone to believe that they must "fire from the hip" to keep order, prevent problems, get a particular job done, or create dramatic changes in the family or business. Firing from the hip also happens to reinforce positional authority while weakening personal power. Usually these people would be better served to explore their anxiety about their use of power, and thoroughly survey the opinions of everyone involved about necessary changes in the group. As I've stated before, EP does not require the surrender of authority—but it can augment personal power sufficiently to make positional power virtually unnecessary.

I've mentioned one method for accelerating the pace of EP itself, the empathic guessing of others' feelings and viewpoints when they are slow to express themselves. This should be used primarily as a means of being helpful, however, not merely for the purpose of speeding things along (or unethically trying to persuade someone that they really want what *you* want). In some circumstances you may find that you can greatly abbreviate Phase 2, the expression of your own viewpoint, particularly when others have the strongest or least expressed feelings about the situation at hand and your viewpoint is well-known.

Finally, you are more likely to use bits and pieces of EP in your real conversations than the full step-by-step agenda that is presented in this book. Sometimes your meticulous restatement of a single, highly sensitive, and long-misunderstood point of conflict between you and another person will have miraculous effects in improving your relationship and accelerating problem solving. And sometimes the mere *intent* to pursue understanding will inaugurate an empathic and productive conversation that constitutes "ethical persuasion" without following all of the steps of the method. In general, I think the problem of finding the time to pursue understanding is solved mostly by deciding that we want mutual understanding before, and more than, anything else.

EP in Group Situations

Because of its emphasis on the intensive exchange, restatement, and mutual understanding of opinions and feelings between people, Ethical Persuasion may seem too unwieldy to apply to group situations, in which four or more people must make decisions or solve problems together. Indeed, EP should not be mistaken for a new kind of parliamentary procedure, or even an etiquette of communication to be applied to every kind of human encounter. EP is specifically designed for use in *difficult* communications that have either become emotionally charged or threaten to become so. Thus, to an EP practitioner the signal for initiation of the process will always be the emergence of strong, disruptive (or potentially disruptive) feelings in anyone in a conversation.

At times, EP can be still be productively pursued in a one-on-one fashion within a group. My friend Craig, the business consultant mentioned earlier in this chapter, once had the occasion to use EP this way while helping the board of directors of a public school system devise a strategic plan for the future of their schools. After several meetings with about ten school board members, it became apparent that the proceedings were being held up by one member in particular, a woman who raised one objection after another to the planning process, much to the exasperation of her colleagues. Proclaiming that she felt it necessary to stand up for minority interests who were being underrepresented in the proceedings, she was in fact receiving the lion's share of attention from everyone. Since the attention was increasingly negative, however, the political agenda she spoke for was actually suffering.

Sensing that the objecting board member felt angry about being ignored at a feeling level, Craig finally interrupted the group process to ask the entire board if he could pursue a better understanding of the woman's viewpoint one-on-one, while everyone else witnessed their conversation. With unanimous consent, Craig then embarked on a careful application of Phase 1 to the woman's concerns, drawing out and restating her viewpoints one at a time, gradually proceeding to deeper and deeper levels of her emotional experience. Within half an hour, the woman was in tears as she revealed to Craig and her colleagues the private anger and frustration she had long felt as a minority political activist, and even how some of her frustration was linked to her early family experience. The other school board members were transfixed. When the woman felt calm and Craig had proved to her that he understood the range of feelings she brought to the issues at hand, everyone took a break before resuming their work together.

Pursuing only Phase 1 of EP with the woman school board member took time, but Craig felt that much more time was saved in the ensuing planning sessions. The woman's political concerns did not disappear, nor did she cease expressing them, but she seemed better able to share the floor equally with everyone and showed a distinct improvement in listening and communication skills.

This is a demonstration of the fact that the personal is political in a way that we often ignore in group proceedings. Presuming that everyone is equally "rational," we plunge into public discussions and disputes that may in fact be heavily influenced and distorted by the unexpressed, feeling-based prejudices of any number of individuals involved. When personal feelings do erupt in public meetings, there will often be an immediate effort to quash their expression and get back to "relevant issues."

Of course, we can't turn all policy meetings into group therapy sessions, and that's not what I'm advocating. From an Ethical Persuasion perspective, however, the interplay of personal feelings and public politics cannot be fruitfully ignored. It takes some experience and expertise to apply EP to group dynamics in the way that Craig did with the school board, but much the same effect could probably have been achieved by another board member privately pursuing EP with the upset woman. Even in large organizations, the vast majority of important communications actually occur on a one-to-one basis.

After a while, EP becomes an instinctive way of relating for its practitioners, and their personal power as effective communicators makes them natural leaders and group facilitators. The technique of EP can be creatively modified for groups by skilled practitioners, for its philosophy is always relevant to any kind of challenging communications.

Devising EP Surveys

An adaptation of Ethical Persuasion that can be useful in larger organizations is the survey or opinion poll, as long as it is intelligently conducted and its results given serious attention. A young woman I know who heads a department of five or six people within a medium-sized public interest agency initiated such a survey to help the group's executives better understand the grumblings and complaints that seemed to be surfacing constantly from frontline employees, albeit without getting the higher-ups' serious attention or having any effect on the internal policies of the organization.

"The real problems in this agency may be bad," this courageous manager warned her superiors, "but the rumors are worse. Let me gather some hard data about what people are feeling like on the job every day, and what ideas they have about internal policy changes they'd like to see. And give me a guarantee that the results of the survey will be discussed by everyone in open department meetings that you guys participate in. The fact is that this agency is headed for some big changes; all of us department heads can feel the ground quaking under our feet. We need your support to grasp what's going on and get a handle on it before we're all overwhelmed."

Some of the agency executives were initially reluctant to try out such an innovative measure, but eventually this manager's idea—essentially to initiate Phase 1 of EP on paper with a large group of employees—was put into effect and resulted in a number of policy changes within the organization (including the voluntary reduction of the CEO's salary in line with an agency-wide budget crunch). With her minimal positional power, this manager could have induced none of these changes in the organization on her own. By instrumenting a collective expression of employees' concerns, she helped turn random, chaotic complaints into an organized, constructive influence that the agency's executives could not sensibly ignore.

To be useful as "EP on paper," several important concerns must be addressed in creating and conducting such a survey. First, its questions ideally should originate mostly from the lower levels of an organization and should preferably be written by a small, democratically chosen group of people. Second, the survey should ask not just for superficial complaints or suggested policy changes, but also for thoughtful feedback on "quality of work life" issues —such as levels of anxiety or enjoyment normally experienced in the professional environment, the quality of work relationships within and between all organizational levels, and the respondents' feelings about coming to work every day. (In most cases, surveys should not require individual identification of respondents.)

Finally, the mechanisms for collating, sharing, and discussing the results of such a survey should be firmly and publicly established *before* it is conducted. This is equivalent to an organization-wide commitment to complete Phase 1 of EP and initiate Phase 2, in the form of open discussions between employees, managers, and executives. From that point on, EP could be applied to any particular point of discussion in any group meeting format.

The reason for clearly establishing beforehand what will be done with the survey results is to make it difficult for managers or executives to seize, withhold, or alter survey results they find unsettling—as our federal government has been known to do with expensive studies whose conclusions happen to contradict the political beliefs of the administration that commissions the studies in the first place! Of course, the idea of the survey can be easily adapted for all kinds of groups and organizations, including schools, hospitals, small businesses, governmental agencies, neighborhood or activist groups, halfway houses, and even large families. In a supposedly free and democratic country, it is surprising how much we still depend on hierarchical and authoritarian organizational structures to get things done and make the countless daily decisions that determine the nature of our culture. As democracy and the free market sweep away the inefficient institutions of Eastern Europe, it's high time that democracy and ethical communication sweep away the antiquated decision-making processes of Western business and government.

Can EP Be Dangerous?

I would be remiss not to discuss situations that are so difficult that it might be dangerous to initiate Ethical Persuasion—for instance, in an encounter between a battered wife and her violent husband. If the wife attempted to pursue Phase 1 of EP on her own, probing her husband's volcanic, distorted emotions without a witness, counselor, or safe environment, then she could conceivably leave herself open to further abuse. Other situations in which physical violence is imminent could obviously be too volatile for the initiation of EP.

However, it's important to remember that EP is a value-driven approach to communication that is dedicated to pursuing respect, understanding, caring, and fairness *for everyone involved*. With rare exceptions, anyone who knowingly makes themselves subject to physical attack while attempting to pursue understanding is violating the values of self-respect, fairness, and care for oneself. A battered wife who wants to change the nature of her communication with her husband will first have to serve her self-respect by removing herself to a safe place, or pursuing EP only with the assistance of a counselor or witness from outside the family. Since most people who are chronically victimized suffer from a long-standing deficit of self-respect and self-care, their first step into EP would best be taken with a trained counselor—for the purpose of understanding themselves and their own feelings—well before they attempt to use the process with a troubled and abusive person.

Thus, Ethical Persuasion is likely to be dangerous only when pursued as a conversational technique stripped of the values it is meant to serve—which would make it *un*ethical, of course. It's easy to imagine how the EP technique could be corrupted to serve unethical ends: a glib, articulate person could manipulate someone unsure of herself into believing that she is being thoroughly understood when in fact her point of view is not being seriously considered, or worse, she is being fed ideas or feelings that the manipulator wants her to think are her own. From there it's a short trip to getting the victim to do something that the manipulator wants.

This has been a ploy of seducers, salesmen, and advertisers since time immemorial, and the mere technique of EP is no more charlatan-proof than any other approach to communication. But most of us have some internal radar for the detection of manipulation, an early warning system that improves with maturity, experience, and sincerity in our relationships. The better we are at pursuing Ethical

Persuasion, as a whole and healthy approach to positive self-change and genuine understanding, the less likely we are to fall prey to those who would misuse our trust.

When EP Is Challenged

A couple who previewed early drafts of this book and began to apply Ethical Persuasion to their own communication difficulties reported an experience that may crop up for other EP novices. During an argument the husband suddenly altered its course by attempting a painstaking restatement of what his wife had been saying. Already flustered and angry, she snapped, "I know what you're trying to do. Just cut it out!" The husband's attempt at Phase 1 floundered, and soon he found himself back in his more familiar pattern of conflict. He later admitted to me that he thought his attempt at EP would have gone better if his application had been more subtle and experienced.

That may be true, but it's not really the point. Behind his wife's "cut it out" message there was probably another message that went something like this: "I'm not going to let you change the rules in the middle of the game. I'm used to our old way of arguing; this new way of not-arguing is too unfamiliar and threatening. I don't know what to expect, and you might be trying to trick me. Or you might really succeed at understanding me better—and what am I supposed to do then?"

Even if one's arguing partner does not know EP, he or she may become suspicious of such a big change in habitual communication patterns and challenge the EP practitioner about what's going on. The awkwardness of trying out a new and artificial way of communication can put one in a highly vulnerable position, in which the temptation to revert to old habits can be overwhelming. If so, one can always try EP again later. To hold on to EP in this kind of situation, one might jump ahead momentarily to some Phase 2 self-explanation:

"Look, I know that what I'm doing seems strange and out of character for me. I am using a deliberate approach to trying to understand you, and I may not be very good at it yet. I can certainly understand that it may seem like a trick or manipulation to you. It feels pretty awkward to me, but that's not the same as it being a trick. I'm actually trying to change the way I talk with you because I'm tired of arguing. So I'm really trying to teach myself to change, and to listen and understand better at this very moment. Can you bear with me while I'm learning to do this?"

The advantage of Ethical Persuasion over many other methods of negotiation is that it doesn't rely on subliminal signals or concealed manipulations of conversation. Thus the practitioner can freely admit not only the use of the technique, but also any awkwardness or vulnerability that may be felt while attempting it. If someone forces you to confess that you are trying out a new and challenging means of communication devoted to the values of respect, understanding, caring, and fairness, then so be it. You may just turn another's suspicion into curiosity, cooperation, and even admiration. Then you will have discovered for yourself what every EP practitioner can learn: behind the greatest difficulties in communication lie the best opportunities for profound mutual understanding and personal growth.

Epilogue:
Ethical Persuasion and
The Human Future

As the manuscript for this book was being finished, the worst riots in America's history broke out in Los Angeles after the controversial courtroom acquittal of four police officers who had been videotaped beating an African-American motorist named Rodney King. Five days of arson, looting, and violence in Los Angeles and elsewhere made it plain that we are far from solving our long-standing problems of race relations and economic inequities.

There may have been one cause of the original violence that is more subtle than the others, but it is no less pervasive in our society. In the May 3, 1992, San Diego edition of the *Los Angeles Times*, columnist Tony Perry reported on a public address given by Norman Stamper, executive assistant police chief in San Diego, two days after the riots broke out. As Perry wrote:

Stamper, who has tried to "demilitarize" the San Diego PD, said the paramilitary structure of most police departments, where cops are told to take orders and keep their mouths shut, breeds anger in the ranks:

"My theory is that every third blow of the baton, every fourth kick to the ribs of Rodney King, was a shot at [police chief] Daryl Gates or a sergeant or a captain or some other functionary of the Los Angeles Police Department who made the mistake of treating a grown-up professional police officer like a dependent, 3-year-old child."

Stamper's analysis is certainly plausible, and reveals the direct but not always apparent link between the quality of interpersonal relationships in professional environments like a police department and the broader social problems of bigotry and violence.

The history of humanity suggests that we are inevitably evolving toward the establishment of universal democracy in our governments, social institutions, and economic life. Yet our progress in fulfilling the democratic instinct has been haphazard, painful, and slow, with many lapses backward into oppression, totalitarianism, and the rule of privilege over the rule of equality.

The struggle of humanity toward democracy can be compared to the struggle of individual human beings toward their own spiritual maturity: We know deep within that our well-being and happiness depend on intimacy, fairness, and communion with each other, but the temptation to react to life's daily difficulties with blame, self-defensiveness, and power-grabbing seems irresistible. It is difficult to imagine the whole human race evolving toward a peaceful and equitable future if we cannot feel ourselves growing more respectful, understanding, caring, and fair in our everyday relationships.

But human beings have an evolutionary advantage that other animals do not: *we can observe our own behavior and learn how to change it.* It's hard, but we can do it. The modern psychological era has brought great advances in our capacity to self-observe, with somewhat less progress in actually learning how to change our ways of thinking and handling our feelings. But it is clear that what a number of modern thinkers call "conscious evolution" is within our grasp. We *can* accelerate the psychological and spiritual maturing of our species by ethical decision making, courageous experimentation, and freely sharing our knowledge.

Teaching and writing about Ethical Persuasion is my own small contribution to our conscious evolution, and it is my sincere hope that trying it out and refining it in your relationships speeds up your progress toward personal fulfillment, intimacy, and democracy in your daily experience. When it seems too tough, remember that EP is an ongoing *process of growth,* not a test of your character at the moment.

Should you falter at giving someone a fair hearing—or find it too exasperating to restate their feelings and opinions—or discover that you're too confused and upset to state your own viewpoint sensibly—try to forgive yourself in the moment so that you can resume the all-important work of pursuing understanding as soon as possible. When others seem to fail, give them the time and opportunity to try again, too. And when you succeed at solving problems and deepening your relationships in the face of serious difficulties of communication, congratulate yourself and your partners on your good work. It's no small matter to bring the human future of democracy, peace, and spiritual fulfillment one step closer.